This exhibition and catalogue are supported by grants from The Pew Memorial Trust and the Commonwealth of Pennsylvania Council on the Arts.

Initial funding was also provided by Fulton Bank, Lancaster; Sperry New Holland; Commonwealth National Bank, Lancaster; First Federal Savings and Loan Association of Lancaster; Hamilton Bank, Lancaster; and American Bank and Trust Company of Pennsylvania.

Pennsylvania Modern: Charles Demuth of Lancaster

Betsy Fahlman

Philadelphia Museum of Art

Distributed by the
University of Pennsylvania Press

Cover: Charles Demuth, **End of the Parade:
Coatesville, Pa. (The Milltown)**
1920 (no. 15)

Philadelphia Museum of Art
July 16–September 11, 1983

The Heritage Center of Lancaster County,
Lancaster, Pennsylvania
October 1–November 13, 1983

Museum of Art, Carnegie Institute, Pittsburgh
November 23, 1983—January 22, 1984

Edited by Susan Webb Soltys
Designed by Laurence Channing
Composition by John C. Meyer & Son, Philadelphia
Printed by Baum Printing, Inc., Philadelphia

Distributed by the University of Pennsylvania Press
3933 Walnut Street
Philadelphia, PA 19104

Library of Congress Cataloging in Publication Data
Fahlman, Betsy.
   Pennsylvania modern : Charles Demuth of Lancaster

   "July 16–September 11, 1983."
   Bibliography: p.
   1. Demuth, Charles, 1883–1935—Exhibitions.
2. Artists—Pennsylvania—Biography. 3. Lancaster (Pa.)—
Biography. I. Demuth, Charles, 1883–1935. II. Philadelphia
Museum of Art. III. Title.
N6537.D445A4   1983   759.13   83-8116
ISBN 0-87633-054-5   (Philadelphia Museum of Art)
ISBN 0-8122-1158-8   (University of Pennsylvania Press)

Contents

The century that has passed since the birth of Charles Demuth at 109 North Lime Street in Lancaster, Pennsylvania, has served to establish and intensify the admiration accorded his work, but, oddly, has brought his admirers little closer to an understanding of this elegant, self-deprecating figure. Five years older than his friend Marcel Duchamp, six years younger than Joseph Stella, who shared Demuth's fascination with industrial subject matter, he was at ease in the modernist circles of both New York and Paris, yet maintained a large measure of independence. Observers have often noted the surprising persistence within Demuth's oeuvre of quite diverse modes of working: the fluid washes and undulating lines of his watercolor studies of acrobats or flowers contrast with the crystalline arcs, lines, and planes of the architectural subjects. His love of Fragonard and El Greco emerges in his rendering of the lithe bodies of vaudeville dancers; his respect for Cézanne and the Cubists informs the delicate yet precise geometry of his paintings of Lancaster buildings. A friend of writers as well as painters, Demuth shared the keen eye of William Carlos Williams, Marianne Moore, and Gertrude Stein, and it seems likely that their clear, clean, and disjointed phrases may in turn have influenced his own art. Yet when he turned his hand to illustration, he chose the dense, rich prose of Henry James and the violent drama of Edgar Allan Poe, for which he drew scenes peopled with disturbing, often sinuous figures.

Demuth therefore presents a puzzling comparison with his fellow students at the Pennsylvania Academy of the Fine Arts, Charles Sheeler and Morton Schamberg, both about his own age. Sharing Sheeler's attachment to the decorative arts and architecture of rural Pennsylvania, and both artists' decisive absorption of the lessons of European modernism, Demuth nonetheless continued to pursue his range of styles and subject matter in contrast to the more rigorous and single-minded pursuit of machine imagery by Schamberg and the precise delineation of rural and industrial buildings by Sheeler. Limiting himself to no single vision, Demuth accorded admiration freely to the work of others: the brilliant and energetic watercolors of John Marin, the paintings of Georgia O'Keeffe, the untiring efforts of Alfred Stieglitz on behalf of the European and American avant-garde. He was one of a handful of his contemporaries to recognize Duchamp's *Large Glass* as "the great picture of our time."* Yet Demuth's own masterpieces, the architectural paintings that now look so classical in their refinement, waited several decades for their reticent beauty to be fully appreciated.

It seems particularly fitting that Demuth's centenary be celebrated in Philadelphia, Lancaster, and Pittsburgh, three cities that together span his native state. His studies at the Pennsylvania Academy, his fascination with the factory landscape of industrial Pennsylvania, and his abiding attachment to Lancaster nourished a rare talent. We owe the initiation of this project to the enthusiasm of Mr. and Mrs. Gerald Lestz, the warm support and encouragement of our colleagues in Lancaster and Pittsburgh, and the timely contribution of a number of banks and other businesses in the Lancaster area. We are grateful to Dr. Betsy Fahlman, herself a former resident of Lancaster, who accepted the challenge of writing the catalogue and who organized the exhibition with the collaborative efforts of Ann Percy, Associate Curator of Drawings, Christine Armstrong, Assistant Curator, and Denise Thomas, Associate Conservator of Art on Paper. Without the generosity of the lenders, who graciously parted with cherished objects, some well known, others shown here for the first time, the exhibition would not have been possible; its realization has been handsomely supported by grants from the Commonwealth of Pennsylvania Council on the Arts and The Pew Memorial Trust.

Anne d'Harnoncourt
The George D. Widener Director
Philadelphia Museum of Art

*Demuth to Alfred Stieglitz, February 5, 1928 or 1929, Collection of American Literature, The Beinecke Rare Book and Manuscript Library, Yale University, New Haven, Conn.

This exhibition marks the one hundredth anniversary of Charles Demuth's birth in Lancaster, Pennsylvania, and is the first to examine his personal and artistic relationship to Lancaster thoroughly. In spite of the changes made in the half century since his death, much of the Lancaster that he knew still exists, presenting an unusual opportunity to study the artist in the context in which he lived. The artist's house stands next to his family's tobacco shop, which is still in business. Demuth's house on East King Street will soon be opened as a museum by the Demuth Foundation. Many buildings that inspired his paintings remain, as do the local farm markets that provided fruit and flowers for his still lifes. The Fulton Opera House, where he enjoyed vaudeville entertainment, continues to present theatrical performances. Many people who knew Demuth and his family still reside in the city. The will of his mother, Augusta, may be examined at the Lancaster County Courthouse, a few blocks from Demuth's home, and the offices of the lawyer who served as the executor of her estate are next door to the tobacco shop. The courthouse was photographed by Demuth's father, Ferdinand, and later inspired one of Charles Demuth's paintings. Local residents still possess cherished Demuth memorabilia. Thus, much of the fabric of the town that nurtured and inspired Demuth is still intact. Modern intrusions scarcely spoil the sense of his presence in Lancaster, reinforcing an observation made by Marsden Hartley in a tribute he wrote after Demuth's death in 1935: "Charles has only just gone." The works assembled for this exhibition give a strong sense of Demuth's relationship to Lancaster. They depict or were inspired by Lancaster subjects, or remained in Lancaster collections for a considerable time.

This exhibition owes an enormous debt to Gerald and Margaret Lestz of Lancaster, whose devoted and longstanding interest in the artist launched the project. I have greatly appreciated the ongoing encouragement and support of Ann Percy of the Philadelphia Museum of Art, whose staff has made my involvement with the exhibition a particularly gratifying experience. Christine Armstrong cheerfully and efficiently took over for Ann Percy while she was on sabbatical, patiently handling innumerable details. Anne d'Harnoncourt, Director, has enthusiastically backed the project, providing helpful editorial suggestions and working hard to secure key loans. I would like to thank Rick Stewart of Williams College, who kindly permitted me to read chapters of his unpublished dissertation on Charles Sheeler and William Carlos Williams. His insightful views of the period in which Demuth worked have significantly shaped my perception of the artist. Emily Farnham was helpful in supplying necessary information. Alvord Eiseman has been most cooperative in responding to many inquiries and in generously sharing with me the abundant fruits of his research. My research would not have been possible without the aid of a number of Lancaster residents, and I would like to thank Harris Arnold, John Aungst, Edward Brubaker, Dorothea Demuth, Brad Dewey, Jean and Eberhard Gromoll, John Ranck, John Snyder, Pauline Stauffer, Gordon Wickstrom, and Bob Wiebe. I am happy to acknowledge the assistance of the following: Dennis R. Anderson; Kathleen Burnside and Mrs. M. P. Naud of Hirschl & Adler Galleries; Courtney Donnell of the Art Institute of Chicago; S. Lane Faison, Jr., of Williams College; Catherine Glasgow of the Columbus Museum of Art; Lise Holst of the Williams College Museum of Art; Liz Jarvis; Antoinette Kraushaar of Kraushaar Galleries; Grete Meilman of Sotheby Parke Bernet; Betty Romanella and Catherine Stover of the Pennsylvania Academy of the Fine Arts; Roberta K. Tarbell; Betty-Bright P. Low and Richmond D. Williams of the Eleutherian Mills Historical Library; Don Winer of the William Penn Memorial Museum; and Judith Zilczer of the Hirshhorn Museum. Numerous collectors, galleries, and museums have kindly responded to my inquiries, and to them I also owe a great debt.

Betsy Fahlman
Assistant Professor of Art History
Old Dominion University

When in 1929 Charles Demuth, in response to the question "What do you look forward to?" posed by *The Little Review*, replied, "the past,"[1] his reply was not entirely whimsical. Although he had by then established his reputation as one of the most important American modernist painters, he was nevertheless deeply rooted in the heritage of his native Lancaster, Pennsylvania. Through his family and surroundings he was drawn to such diverse sources as old-fashioned flower painting or Pennsylvania German fraktur, yet he espoused the most advanced modern styles of his time.

Previous studies have not ignored Demuth's strong Lancaster heritage; they have tended to concentrate, however, on his relationship to contemporary artistic movements in New York and Paris. In order to gain a balanced understanding of Demuth's development and to arrive at a full appreciation of his works, a consideration of his Lancaster experience is essential. Just as Demuth's contact with modern art in New York and in Europe was instrumental in developing his style, his Lancaster experiences provided the basis for his visual orientation as well as for his characteristic subject matter.

Demuth's career presents a series of intriguing paradoxes and a combination of episodes that served to produce a richly subtle and fascinating body of work. In his art he was able to balance a deeply rooted admiration for one of the most historic areas in the United States with an enthusiasm for and keen understanding of the most advanced developments in American and European art. Demuth was an urbane man whose friends included Marcel Duchamp, Marsden Hartley, and Alfred Stieglitz; yet for various reasons he spent most of his life working in a provincial locale. The clean lines of the older buildings and industrial architecture of his native city exerted a strong visual impact on Demuth that remained fundamental to his vision even when he did work elsewhere, such as Bermuda, Gloucester, or Provincetown. Despite spending a large part of his life away from the main centers of the art world, he nonetheless made a seminal contribution to the history of American art. As a major American modernist, his visual language intriguingly combines aspects of American Regionalism and Precisionism.

Lancaster (see fig. 2) was Demuth's lifelong home, and the artist had many ties there. He was born there, he painted many of his major works in his second-floor studio overlooking the garden of his family's home, and it was in Lancaster that he died at the age of fifty-two. Described as "a town of considerable old-world charm"[2] by the art critic Henry McBride, Lancaster first achieved prominence as the largest inland city of the thirteen colonies and boasts rich historical associations. What might be viewed as its narrow limitations actually represented for Demuth financial, physical, and emotional security: "the solid background of his rich simplicity," according to Marsden Hartley.[3] As James Thrall Soby perceptively observed, "His art reflects this security and permanence, not in its subject matter so much as in its subtle, aristocratic air of sanctuary and withdrawal."[4] The city remained for the artist both a source of creative inspiration and of stability. His modernist idiom provided the perfect expression for rendering not only the crisp forms, unadorned clarity, and precision of Lancaster architecture, but also for depicting the fruits and flowers of the city's markets and the vaudeville troupes that performed there.

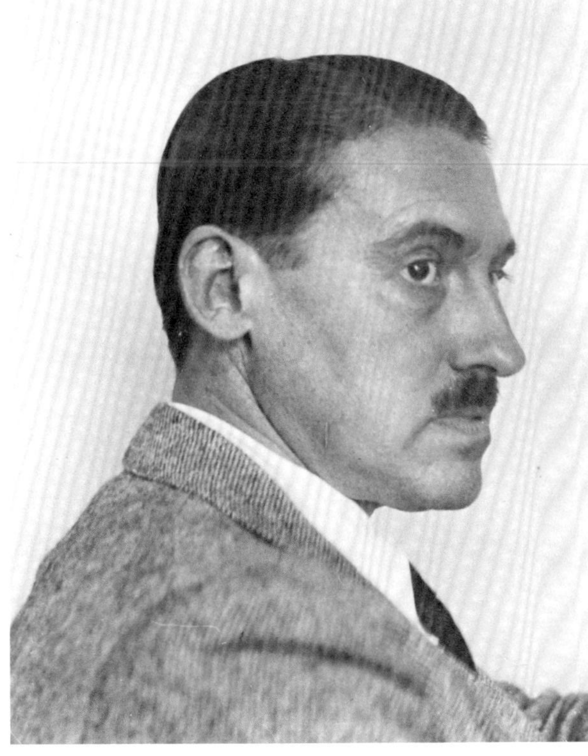

Fig. 1. Charles Demuth, by Dorothy Norman, c. 1930 (Philadelphia Museum of Art. From the Collection of Dorothy Norman. 68-114-29)

Lancaster turned out to be ideally situated for the artist's needs: isolated enough to serve as a refuge from the outside world, but accessible to the art world in Philadelphia and New York. Rita Wellman, a classmate of Demuth's from the Pennsylvania Academy of the Fine Arts, described the arrangement of Demuth's life: "Charles Demuth paints in Lancaster. He does nothing else there. When he feels he wants to see people he comes to New York. After three or four days of seeing people he decides it is time to go back to Lancaster. . . . He is not home-loving, nor anti-social. Lancaster fits, and when something fits it is a good idea to keep to it, if you have work to do."[5]

After his death, a number of Demuth's friends maintained that he disliked Lancaster, and the recollections of the painter George Biddle are among the most extreme: "He loathed and was bored to death with Lancaster and the Pennsylvania Dutch. He was one himself."[6] Demuth's true feelings for the city, however, were never that simple; his seeming unsociability there had a great deal to do with his serious illness and his need for privacy in which to paint. Demuth himself maintained, in a letter to Stieglitz from Lancaster, "I'll stay here and work,—I don't see anything else. I like a few places and a few people but I see them seldom. Perhaps I wouldn't work at all if I did,—still, I don't like most of my work, and maybe that's what keeps me working."[7] His friend Susan Watts Street later recalled, "In Lancaster Demuth didn't mix with people much. He would shut himself off, especially after the diabetes came, and work."[8] His illness forced him to seclude himself from New York society as well.

While his circle of Lancaster friends was never a large one, he maintained contact with several people who had been his friends since childhood, thoughtfully remembering them with presents of drawings when they married. Most significant of his Lancaster intimates was Robert Evans Locher (1888–1956), who remained his closest lifelong friend. Locher was also a native Lancastrian, and the two were childhood playmates. Locher, too, was an artist, although he specialized in producing fashionable interior schemes in the Art Deco style as well as theater and costume designs and Beardsleyesque illustrations for *Vanity Fair*. Like Demuth, Locher was involved with several avant-garde magazines, including

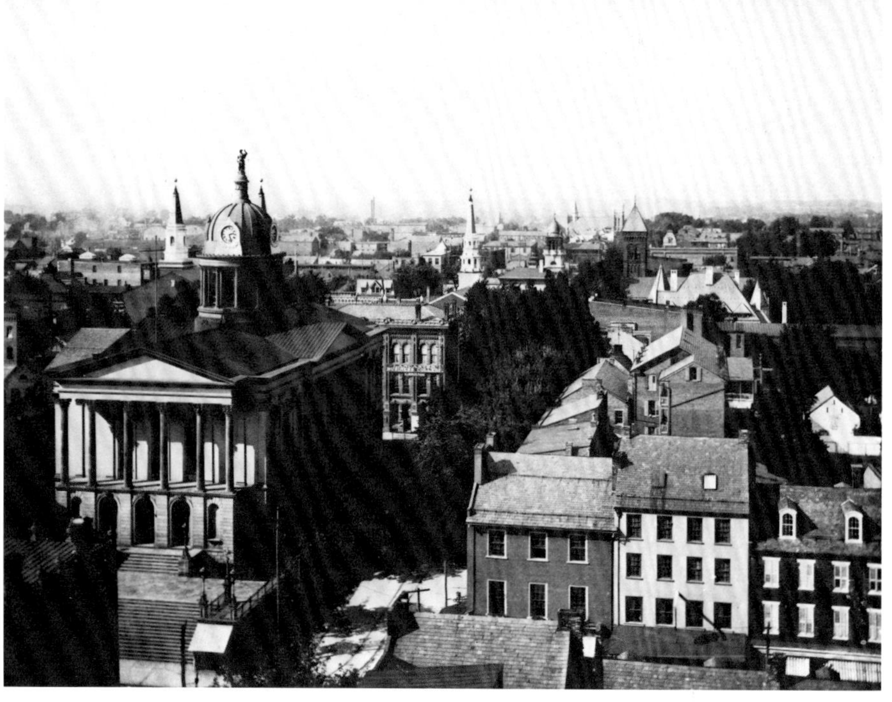

Fig. 2. View of Lancaster, looking north from Trinity Lutheran Church. Published in *Art Work of Lancaster* (Chicago: W. H. Parish Publishing Co., 1892)

the short-lived *Rogue*, for which he produced illustrations. Locher's design commissions came from a variety of fashionable patrons, including Juliana Force, the first director of the Whitney Museum of American Art, as well as the decorator Elsie DeWolf, and Florenz Ziegfeld, creator of the Ziegfeld Follies. He also planned the interiors of the first Whitney Museum building, on Eighth Street. Locher's designs, featured in such widely circulated magazines as *Vogue* and *House and Garden*, were executed as far afield as Havana. He and Demuth shared many friends, including the New York painter Florine Stettheimer, who with her two sisters Ettie and Carrie conducted a lively artistic salon, the writer Muriel Draper, and Gertrude Stein. Locher saw the latter two on his frequent trips to Paris during the 1920s, where he worked for the designer Paul Poiret, among others. Gertrude Stein also knew Locher's wife, Beatrice, and wrote a word portrait of her (see no. 17).

Later, Demuth became close to Darrell Larsen, who had come to Lancaster in 1927 to teach drama at Franklin and Marshall College. A talented man with discriminating taste and high standards, Larsen managed to establish the college's Green Room Theatre as a major local forum, especially when the Fulton Opera House fell into disuse during the Depression. In 1928 Larsen, who was also involved in community theatrical ventures, incorporated a Byzantine door and window design by Demuth and Robert Groezinger in sets for a play he directed for the Drama Club of Lancaster at Brinkman Hall, an auditorium not far from Demuth's house. Larsen and Demuth frequently saw each other socially, and together they were regular guests at the home of Jack and Blanche Steinman, prominent Lancaster citizens.

When Demuth invited his New York friends to visit him at home, he referred to Lancaster with affectionate humor as "the province."[9] But Lancaster could hardly be regarded as remote, since regular train service connected it with Philadelphia in an hour and a half, and the artist could travel on to New York within another two hours. Demuth took full advantage of his proximity to these two cities, a convenience that enabled him to visit friends regularly and to remain in close contact with artistic developments, and his friends traveled to Lancaster to see him as well. Demuth's visitors included a distinguished list of personalities, such as Henry McBride, Adolphe Borie, Georgia O'Keeffe, Alfred Stieglitz, Charles Daniel, Albert E. Gallatin, William Carlos Williams, Albert Barnes, Marsden Hartley, and George Biddle.

Visitors to his house were greeted by an interior rather different from that of many of the other older homes in the city. In addition to the family's antiques, Demuth decorated his walls with more modern art, including several watercolors by John Marin, photographs by Man Ray of Beatrice and Robert Locher, a lithograph by Toulouse-Lautrec, paintings by Georgia O'Keeffe and Marsden Hartley, and drawings by Aubrey Beardsley, Louis Bouché, Jules Pascin, and Henri Matisse.

The state of Pennsylvania did not completely ignore the artist during his lifetime, although such recognition came to Demuth infrequently: "We of Philadelphia are so ready to discount the performance of a local prophet," remarked Helen Henderson in 1918. "Now that Demuth has 'arrived' . . . we see nothing of his work in Philadelphia—occasionally a watercolor from his hand might get into the annual exhibition of works in that medium, but if the jury took it, the Hanging Committee took care so to place it that it would be the last thing seen if seen at all. . . . Meanwhile Charles never did more than laugh an amused chuckle at his rating and paint away contentedly."[10] Late in 1912 Demuth served on several committees responsible for organizing the "Loan Exhibition of Historical and Contemporary Portraits Illustrating the Evolution of Portraiture in Lancaster County, Pennsylvania." His own contribution to the exhibition was a conservative student painting, his *Self-Portrait* (no. 1), the only work he exhibited in Lancaster during his lifetime. Other paintings owned by the Demuth family were also lent to this exhibition. In 1919 Demuth was chosen by the Pennsylvania Academy of the Fine Arts, where he had been a student, to serve as a member of the Jury of Selection and Award for their annual exhibition of watercolors. When in 1926 he received a silver medal for his 1925 watercolor *Plums* (Addison Gallery of American Art, Phillips Academy, Andover, Massachusetts; Farnham 1959, painting no. 473) at the Sesqui-Centennial Exposition in Philadelphia, he noted wryly, "It seems funnier to be noticed than not to be."[11] In the same year, he participated in the Academy's Twenty-Fourth Annual Watercolor Exhibition, winning the Dana Watercolor Medal for his *Roses, 1920* or 1926 (Museum of Fine Arts, Boston; Farnham 1959, painting no. 392).

Demuth found one of his most supportive patrons in the Pennsylvania collector Dr. Albert Barnes. Although Barnes's difficult personality sometimes made their relationship uneasy, Demuth did visit Barnes at his home in Merion, near Philadelphia, and they encountered each other in Paris. When they did not see each other, they corresponded. Barnes ultimately acquired about forty works by Demuth, which remain today as part of the Barnes Foundation, Merion. Only one other collector purchased Demuth's work in such quantity: Ferdinand Howald of Columbus, Ohio, who came to own some thirty-five oil and tempera paintings and watercolors. Even Demuth's most loyal supporter, Alfred Stieglitz, never owned so many. Another pair of Philadelphia collectors, Vera and Samuel S. White, 3rd, of Ardmore, also bought nine Demuth works.

The facts of Charles Demuth's life reveal most clearly the kind of continuing and fruitful source of inspiration his native city provided to him. He was born November 8, 1883, in a house at 109 North Lime Street, not far from the center of Lancaster, into a German family that had resided in Pennsylvania since 1735. By the second half of the eighteenth century, his great-great-grandfather, Christopher Demuth (1738–1818), had settled at 114 East King Street in Lancaster, where he established a tobacco shop (fig. 3) in 1770 and later a small snuff factory. The shop, still active today, is the oldest tobacco shop in the United States operated on its original site by descendants of the original owner.[12]

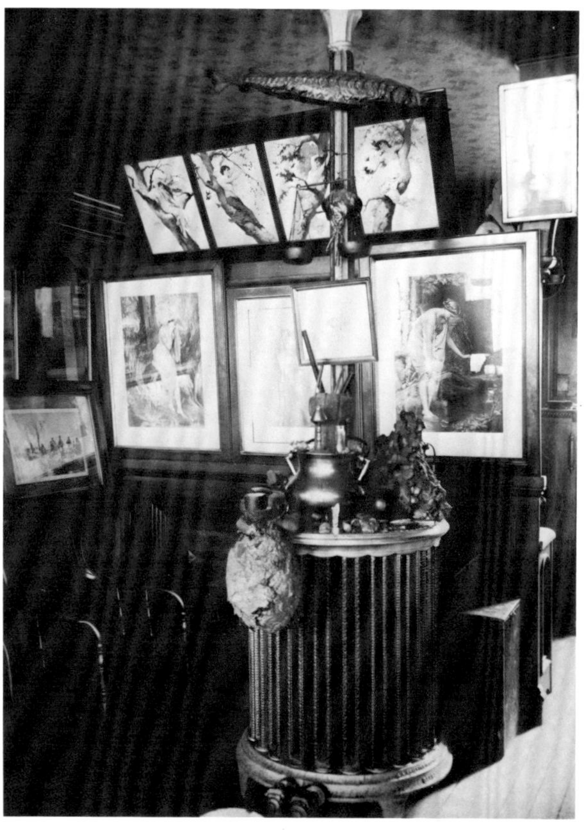

Fig. 3. Interior of Demuth tobacco shop, by Ferdinand Demuth, c. 1900 (Private Collection)

In 1887, when Demuth was four and while he was still living on Lime Street, he suffered the hip injury that left him permanently lame. Two years later his family moved into a nearby house at 118 East King Street, which had previously been occupied by a relative. Built about 1750, the house was two doors from the family's tobacco shop (fig. 4). Demuth continued to live there until his death.

Several Demuth family members were involved in the arts. John Demuth (b. 1770), was a woodcarver who, in addition to executing a number of family portraits, produced a painted wooden statue now titled *The Snuff Taker of Revolutionary Days*, which served as the first sign for the tobacco shop. Two other relatives, Charles Demuth's grandmother Caroline Suzanne Demuth (b. 1812) and Samuel Christopher Demuth (b. 1817), left sketchbooks containing their work, and his aunt Louisa Demuth (b. 1814) painted flowers in watercolor.[13] Further artistic connections may be found with Charles Demuth's great-aunt Sarah Demuth, who married the now-obscure painter Aaron Eshelman (b. 1827), about whom Demuth wrote an appreciative article.[14] Emmanuel Demuth married Margaret Eichholtz, daughter of the well-known Lancaster portrait painter Jacob Eichholtz (1776–1842), whose house was not far from that of the Demuths. By the late nineteenth century, Charles's father Ferdinand A. Demuth (1857–1911), who ran the family business with his brother from 1906, had become an enthusiastic amateur photographer and an active member of the Lancaster Camera Club. A number of Lancaster buildings photographed by his father later served as subjects for Charles Demuth's paintings.

Of all his relatives, the artist's mother, Augusta Buckius Demuth (1856–1943), also of an established Lancaster family, played the most significant role in his life. Although she was not an artist herself, it was she who created the secure and ordered environment necessary for her son to paint. According to Robert Locher's friend Richard Weyand, Demuth referred to his mother as "Augusta the Iron-Clad" and "a ship under full sail,"[15] but he seems to have made these observations with good-natured affection, for he enjoyed a close and supportive relationship with her. Marsden Hartley described Mrs. Demuth with admiration: "His mother must be brought into the picture with tender regard, for she is one of those fine old householders in a small Pennsylvania town, so fastidious about the order of

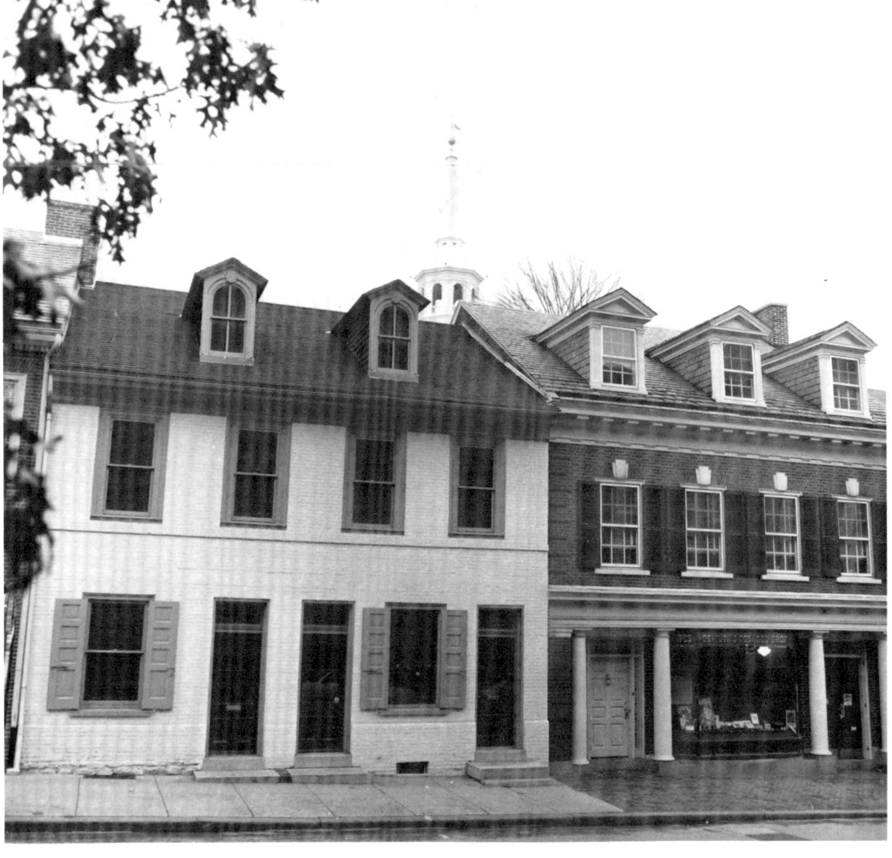

Fig. 4. Exterior of Demuth house and tobacco shop, 1983

her home that she does everything herself as part of the noble rites of existence."[16] Hartley revealed that Charles Demuth did not regret coming home to Lancaster, continuing: "In the midst of this rich domestic milieu Charles was reared, and when he was at home he liked it thoroughly, as when he was abroad he liked the usual variations of such character."[17]

Henry McBride, too, admired Augusta, who at six feet tall appeared to him an "extraordinarily robust mother,"[18] a characteristic observed by William Carlos Williams, who described her as "a horse of a woman, a strange mother for such a wisp of a man."[19] Williams was well aware of the enormously supportive role his mother played for Demuth, once referring to her as his "patron saint,"[20] a term she well deserved for her devoted efforts in carefully weighing her son's food and overseeing his two daily insulin injections after his diabetes was diagnosed. Demuth was occasionally pleased and amused to relay his mother's intuitive observations on the art world when writing to Stieglitz.

Charles Demuth was an only child. His parents did not discourage his early interest in art, and while still young he began receiving art lessons from a number of Lancaster-area residents. The artist painted his earliest extant watercolor when he was thirteen. By the time he was seventeen, he had mastered the techniques of needlepoint and china painting, which he used to decorate teacups, saucers, and plates with flowers. He and his mother transformed needlepoint designs into pillows and chair covers.

In 1899, Demuth entered Franklin and Marshall Academy, graduating in 1901. Upon completing his schooling in Lancaster, he settled in Philadelphia, where he enrolled in art school at the Drexel Institute of Art, Science and Industry. During this period of his earliest formal art classes, he made the acquaintance of William Carlos Williams, who was then studying medicine at the University of Pennsylvania. Williams and Demuth found themselves residents of the same boarding-house on Locust Street, took an instant liking to one another, and thereafter remained close friends. His contact with the poet undoubtedly reinforced the artist's strong literary bent, for Demuth occasionally considered becoming a writer during this period, just as Williams occasionally considered becoming a painter. Demuth never abandoned his interest in writing and throughout his career periodically published on art and other topics.

Demuth entered the Pennsylvania Academy of the Fine Arts in 1905, sporadically attending classes there until 1911, while at the same time continuing to pursue occasional courses at Drexel. His instructors at the Academy included several distinguished teachers, such as Thomas Anshutz, Hugh Breckenridge, Henry McCarter, and William Merritt Chase. Although Demuth's mature style bears little resemblance to that of his teachers, his works from these early years reflect their range of influences, particularly in his realist approach combined with a painterly style. Demuth developed friendships with several of his fellow students. Two, Helen Henderson and Rita Wellman, remained close to him for the rest of his life. Miss Henderson, as a critic for the *Philadelphia Inquirer*, later wrote appreciative articles on the artist. His artist friends in Philadelphia included the painters Adolphe Borie and George Biddle.

In 1904 Demuth made his first trip to Europe, spending several weeks there as a twenty-first birthday present from his parents. Little is known of this trip; it was of short duration and appears to have had little effect on his art. More significant was his trip to Paris in 1907, a prolonged stay of about five months. Although he did little formal painting while he was there, he made many watercolors and sketches, which served as studies for more finished works completed after his return to Lancaster. In style, however, these works remain closely related to those he had already produced during his student years at the Academy. Following his return to the United States in March 1908, he spent the summer at New Hope, a Pennsylvania town not far from Philadelphia which was popular with artists. For several subsequent summers Demuth returned to New Hope, and also traveled to Monhegan Island in Maine, a locale also favored by the noted illustrator Rockwell Kent, and to Lambertville, New Jersey, across the Delaware River from New Hope.

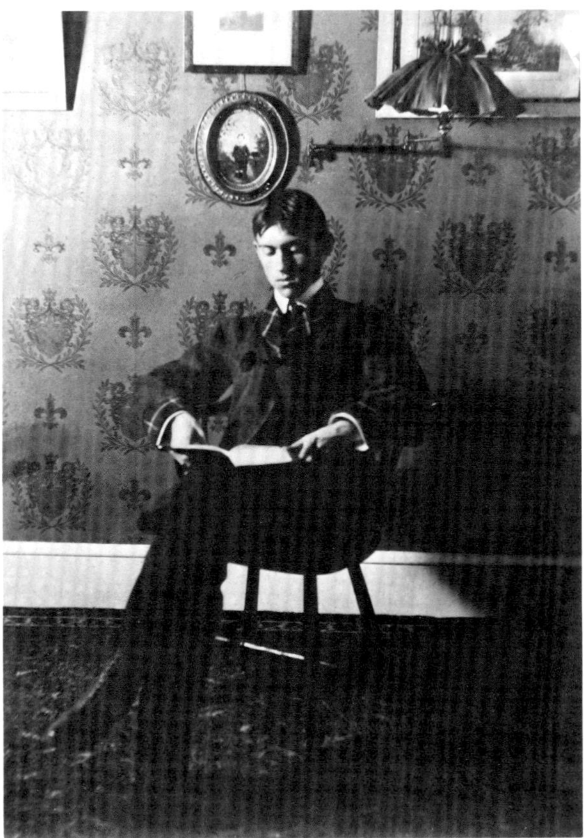

Fig. 5. Charles Demuth at
about age 15, c. 1898
(Dorothea G. Demuth)

Demuth returned to Paris again in December 1912, remaining until the spring of 1914. He soon came into contact with literary and intellectual circles there, meeting the sculptor Jo Davidson as well as Ezra Pound and Gertrude Stein. With the artists Marsden Hartley and Arnold Rönnebeck, he also managed a trip to Berlin. At this time he was more receptive to European modernism than he had been previously, no doubt partly because of the influence of contemporary exhibitions he had seen in New York, and his palette became brighter and his touch more fluid.

Demuth's work was first exhibited in public at the Pennsylvania Academy Annuals of 1907, 1908, and 1911, but after his return to the United States in 1914 he was given his first one-man exhibition, consisting of twenty-five watercolors, at the Daniel Gallery in New York, one of the most avant-garde galleries. He continued to exhibit regularly with the gallery until 1923. The critic Henry McBride, a fellow Pennsylvanian born in West Chester in 1867, favorably reviewed the exhibition[21] and thereafter remained one of the artist's most loyal supporters.

From the time of his first exhibition at the Daniel Gallery in 1914, Demuth was frequently compared to another well-known American watercolorist, John Marin. Both artists were members of the Stieglitz circle, and the painter George Biddle later recalled a comment he claimed Demuth had made to him: "All of us drew our inspiration from the spring of French modernism. John Marin pulled his up in bucketfuls but he spilled much along the way. I had only a teaspoon in which to carry mine; but I never spilled a drop."[22] Indeed, Demuth exercised considerable restraint in his application of watercolor as he carefully worked out compositional problems. He had a high regard for Marin and later painted a poster portrait of him. On the basis of their watercolors, the two artists were regarded by the collector A. E. Gallatin and others by 1927 as "the most important figures in contemporary American painting."[23] It was Henry McBride who resolved the essential problem troubling critics attempting to compare the work of Marin and Demuth: "But can Demuth be modern, you ask, if Marin is?

Why not? The oddest fallacy amid all those that persist is that there must be a formula for modern art. Both men connect with the times, though they connect differently. The submerged, inner life of Marin revolts at science and fights it. But the science that kills Marin keeps Demuth alive. Demuth chants the Hymn Intellectual, as Walt Whitman would say."[24]

Demuth spent the summers of 1915 and 1916 in Provincetown, Massachusetts, a popular vacation spot with Greenwich Villagers since a group of writers "discovered" it in 1911. Demuth's friends there included the painters Carl Sprinchorn, Marsden Hartley, Stuart Davis, and Edward Fisk, as well as critic Helen Henderson. Known by his nickname Deem, the artist enjoyed the relaxed yet stimulating atmosphere of Provincetown in the teens. He came in frequent contact with people involved with the Provincetown Players and acted in a number of amateur theatricals. It was there that he first befriended Susan Watts Street, a young society woman from New York who became one of his most faithful friends and who collected a number of his works. Demuth was especially interested in the old buildings he saw in Provincetown, which continued to serve as subjects for his paintings for years to come, although during this period he painted land-scapes and beach scenes for the most part.

After his summers in Provincetown, Demuth divided his time between New York and Lancaster, traveling to New York almost every week. Usually he stayed at one of two Greenwich Village hotels, the Brevoort or the Lafayette, and during the fall of 1915 he rented a studio on Washington Square South. Demuth enjoyed an active social life in New York, frequenting such popular night spots as Marshall's on West 53rd Street and Barron Wilkins' Little Savoy, first located on West 35th Street and later in Harlem.

The mid- to late teens was an especially rich period for artists in New York City. Following the Armory Show of 1913, America's first large-scale exposure to modern art, there was considerable interest in and discussion of avant-garde art in America. A strong sense of community developed among artists, and the presence of a number of Europeans, including Picabia and Duchamp—temporarily settled in the United States as a result of conditions in Europe brought about by World War I—further inspired Demuth and his contemporaries. Although he had undoubtedly encountered Cubism and other modern art during his trips to Paris, it was during this period that Demuth assimilated these influences to develop his mature style.

His first serious explorations in the Cubist style, a series of paintings depicting architecture and the landscape, were made during the winter of 1916–1917, on a trip to Bermuda with Hartley. The artist responded sympathetically to the geometric lines of Bermuda's colonial buildings, accentuating their angular shapes and sharply defined forms, but fragmenting the forms as if viewing them through a prism. During the summer of 1917, following his return from Bermuda, he visited Gloucester, Massachusetts, which, like Lancaster and Provincetown, had colonial architecture that fascinated him. He continued to experiment with the possibilities of Cubism.

While he was in Bermuda and Gloucester, Demuth had concentrated on architectural views and landscapes; in the late teens he renewed his interest in the figure, embarking on another series of watercolors and drawing treating themes drawn from the vaudeville theater, a subject he had begun depicting in New York in 1915. Although he continued to frequent nightclubs and other entertainments when he was in New York, most of his works based on this theme were executed in Lancaster. Lancaster was an important stop on the vaudeville circuit, and Demuth could attend performances in Lancaster either at the Colonial Theatre or at the Fulton Opera House, each a short distance from his home. He depicted the performances he saw there in the spirit, if not in the styles, of Toulouse-Lautrec and Degas, who had also recorded the world of performers. The spare and fluid lines of Demuth's drawings and watercolors, with their luminous washes, prompted the art critic Willard Huntington Wright to observe in 1917 that "Demuth achieves a delicacy of volumnear poise equal to Matisse's."[25]

During his third stay in Paris, Demuth experienced the first symptoms of what would later be diagnosed as diabetes, but more intense symptoms did not appear until 1920. Despite suffering a number of severe diabetic attacks during the summer of 1920, he recovered sufficiently to return to Paris between August and November of 1921. Demuth was delighted to be back in Europe, writing to Stieglitz upon his arrival in London, where he spent a short time before proceeding to France: "I wonder if it will ever happen in the land of the free?—or, is it happening? I never knew Europe was so wonderful,—and, never knew, really,—not so surely, that New York, if not the country, has something not found here."[26]

Demuth deplored the general lack of support for art in America, but at the same time he realized that there were also tremendous opportunities for an artist, and never considered becoming an expatriate. Although he cherished his time in Paris, he realized that America was necessary for his work, as he wrote to Stieglitz from Lancaster: "What work I do will be done here; terrible as it is to work in this 'our land of the free'. . . . Together we will add to the American Scene."[27] "I fell 'in' America,—even though it's [sic] insides are empty. Maybe I can help fill them."[28]

The artist's illness became more debilitating during the spring of 1922, and he was admitted to the Physiatric Sanitorium in Morristown, New Jersey. Initially he was treated through a program of drastically reduced diet; later he began to receive insulin injections. Insulin had just been discovered to be effective in the treatment of diabetes, and Demuth was one of the first in the United States to receive the drug. His stay at the sanitorium was cheered by visits from his friends, including Susan Watts Street and William Carlos Williams. He kept in touch with others by letter. By July he was able to return to Lancaster, although later attacks forced him to be readmitted to the sanitorium during the spring of 1923.

In 1920, shortly before his health had deteriorated more severely, Demuth had embarked on a series of architectural paintings inspired by the buildings of Lancaster. No human figures appear in any of the architectural works, as the artist was more intrigued by the visual rhythms and formal relationships created by the smokestacks, billowing smoke, and geometric shapes of the buildings. Among the first he presented to the public was a group to which he gave such varied titles as *The Tower: After Sir Christopher Wren* (Columbus Museum of Art); *Waiting; Machinery (For W. Carlos W.)* (The Metropolitan Museum of Art); *End of the Parade: Coatesville, Pa.* (no. 15); *Chimneys, Ventilators or Whatever* (Farnham 1959, painting no. 736); *After Sir Christopher Wren (New England)* (Worcester Art Museum); *Pennsylvania*; and *The Merry Go Round*. These new works were exhibited at the Daniel Gallery in 1920. During this period he executed few of the figurative watercolors that had preoccupied him since the mid-teens, confiding to Henry McBride that he had discontinued painting them because "I simply haven't the strength."[29]

Demuth's new subjects also signaled a shift in technique. Few of his works based on Lancaster architecture are executed in watercolor; oil and tempera became his favorite mediums. In 1927 A. E. Gallatin commented on this new thematic and formal interest: "Demuth evidently came to the conclusion that oil and tempera were more appropriate media for the delineation of lofty chimneys, iron girders and red brick façades than the more fragile medium of water-colour. These unlovely things, belonging so distinctly to our era of commercialism and mass production, have been made lovely by Demuth's rare art. . . . Not only beautiful, on account of their harmony and unity, these paintings of modern industrial America would at times almost seem to strike a note of gaiety. The titles, too, are witty."[30]

Demuth regarded his oils and temperas of industrial themes as major statements. Their creation consumed much of his energy and time and there are relatively few of them. For variety, he continued to return to watercolor throughout this period for other subjects, as he wrote to Stieglitz in 1923: "I've only painted in watercolour; the strain is greater, but, I don't have to return and fuss if it goes bad as one always does in oil or tempera."[31]

Milton Brown and other historians of American art have since agreed that "Demuth's architectural paintings were the earliest, and remain among the finest, examples of American industrial landscapes."[32] But when the artist first exhibited these pieces they were not uniformly well received, as a critic wrote in a review of an exhibition held at the Daniel Gallery in 1922: "Just what Mr. Demuth is driving at we cannot imagine, nor does it much matter, for his rigidly careful drawings of dull objects, though redeemed by an occasional flash of agreeable color, do not seem to us to have any artistic interest whatever."[33] The works the critic was referring to included *Welcome to Our City, Nospmas M. Egiap Nospmas M.* (no. 18), *From the Garden of the Château* (no. 23), *Incense of a New Church* (no. 21), *Modern Conveniences* (Columbus Museum of Art).

Even long after Demuth's death, many critics remained unsympathetic to the architectural works inspired by Lancaster themes, and they continued to feel that these paintings lacked "his emotional insight," and seemed more "like intellectual exercises than deeply felt ideas."[34] However, some critics reacted favorably, as did Henry McBride, who wrote in a review published in 1920 that Demuth's "studies of aspects of New England and Pennsylvania would be quite terrible—if they were not so beautiful."[35] McBride continued to admire these works, writing in another review that appeared in 1923: "He is aware of concrete, of immense, implacable walls of red brick, and of the towering smokestacks which cut more of a figure now than church steeples do—and somehow he doesn't seem to mind being of this period. Fortunate artist. The moment in which the setting sun throws the rubbishy heap of scrap-iron into a puzzlingly suggestive mass of shadow and flicks strange designs upon the flat walls of brick, seems sufficient for him. He makes of it a thing that seems to glorify a subject that the rest of us have been taught to consider ugly."[36] It was many years before other critics wrote in a similarly favorable manner about these works. By 1937, observers such as Edward Alden Jewell had begun to write admiringly of Demuth's architectural paintings, describing several, including *Chimney and Water Tower* (no. 34), *End of the Parade: Coatesville, Pa.* (no. 15), and *My Egypt* (no. 29) as "elaborate dislocations and bizarre reconstructions —with forms broken up, though never disintegrated."[37]

Demuth's works based on the architecture o Lancaster are not easily interpreted. Full of personal meanings for the artist and complex artistic allusions, their stark subject and angula technique appeared stern and unappealing to those who had come to admire the fluidity and the flowing color of his flower and fruit pieces or the lively line and the engaging subject of his vaudeville works. The witty titles of these paintings are often misleading, and few writers have analyzed them beyond amuse- ment over the names, identification of the Lancaster buildings they represent, or gen- eralized acknowledgment of their connections to modern styles. The key to the meaning of these pictures, however, lies in their subject, in their reference to Lancaster.

One of the first art historians to examine the relationship of Demuth's architectural works to the Lancaster buildings that inspired them was S. Lane Faison, Jr., who, comparing certain paintings and photographs of local buildings, concluded that Demuth's paintings were "more faithful to the original motive than their sparse cubist appearance might indicate."[38] His study helpfully identifies many of the specific visual sources for the artist's paintings, but does not explore the underlying intellectual and personal connections fundamental to Demuth' subtle and complex use of his native city as subject.

These highly sophisticated paintings require interpretation on several different levels: their titles are related to the intellectual conundrum favored by Demuth's friend Marcel Duchamp and other Dada artists, but they are more than a display of Demuth's easy familiarity with Duchampian ideas. The titles reflect Demuth's own sense of humor and experience of life; they often refer to books he had read, to parts of the city he knew well, or to ideas he had encountered in New York. Their undeniable humor has diverted attention from the complexity and richness of their associations.

For example, the title of one of his most famous works, *My Egypt* (no. 29), depicting the monumental grain elevators of a local feed company near his home, at once refers to ancient history and to Demuth's own frail health. *Aucassin and Nicolette* (no. 19), on the other hand, reinterprets a French medieval romance architecturally. Visually these paintings relate to modern styles, especially to Cubism, in their inverse formal reductions and broad areas of color, but they depict ordinary vernacular architecture. While the specific buildings depicted are relatively easy to identify, it is less easy to arrive at the significance of the subjects.

These architectural works, based on structures in and near Lancaster, established Charles Demuth as a leading member of the group subsequently known as the Precisionists.[39] According to Patrick Stewart, "Its chief aesthetic source is not so much the worship of the machine, but the adaptation of science-oriented methods to visual perception. This, in turn, leads to what Precisionism in fact was: a fundamental reordering of reality brought about by the rise of an Objectivist aesthetic which can be said to have developed not only in painting, but in literature as well . . . a unified movement in American art and literature that combined an awakening sense of place with a growing objectivist viewpoint."[40] This sense of place was vital for Demuth's art and informs almost all aspects of his painting, since most of his works are strongly related to Lancaster. Gallatin had noted as early as 1922 that "Demuth's drawings of buildings . . . are full of the locality of the scene."[41]

The art of the Precisionists did not exhibit sentimental nostalgia for a simple romanticized past as did that of some of the Regionalists, but, in their dedication to subject matter drawn from local sources, the Precisionists bear intriguing parallels to those artists. Although Demuth's Pennsylvania ties remained strong, he could never be called an American Regionalist: "Precisionism, then, was not literal Regionalism; it was a conscious attempt to summarize the radical notions of form, reality, and place that had concerned many thoughtful artists and writers since the end of the First World War."[42] A modern American artist with strong ties to a rural area was not especially unusual during this era. For instance, Charles Sheeler's long-standing interest in rural American craftsmanship remained an important source for his art. Not only was he inspired by the early farm buildings of Doylestown, Pennsylvania, but he was also interested in the old buildings at Ephrata, Pennsylvania, in Shaker structures, and later in his life, in colonial Williamsburg. Later in their careers, John Marin and Marsden Hartley were intensely affected by the rugged landscape of Maine. Georgia O'Keeffe has spent much of her creative life in the Southwest, producing works that are a powerful blend of realism and abstraction, often inspired by Spanish colonial structures there.

In keeping with the historic surroundings of the town in which he lived, Demuth's home was filled with many reminders of the past. The Demuth family owned many fine pieces of antique furniture, which are listed in the artist's will. Marsden Hartley gave a vivid picture of the family home: "It belongs to the era of shell flowers, wax fruit, painted velvet, bead-encrusted antimacassars, and the usual complement of horsehair, bell pulls, opaque glass, silver lustre, and all the lavish profusion of accessory of such periods."[43] One early Pennsylvania William and Mary–style table owned by the family was of sufficient quality to be accepted into the collection of the Metropolitan Museum of Art in New York following Augusta Demuth's death in 1943. In fact, Demuth was enough of an expert on the subject to be able to advise Walter Arensberg on the purchase of some antiques for his collection.[44] As James Thrall Soby observed, "A regard for the eighteenth century was an essential of Demuth's vision."[45] The comparison that the critic Forbes Watson drew in observing the art of Charles Sheeler could easily be applied to that of Demuth: "Moreover, in the clean-cut fineness, the cool austerity, the complete distrust of superfluities which we find in some pieces of early American furniture, I seem to see the American root of Sheeler's art."[46]

Demuth's architectural paintings were among his last important works. Although he continued to produce throughout the 1920s and early 1930s, his illness, which became more and more of a struggle, often prevented him from working, as he confided to Stieglitz in 1930: "Didn't work at all, but have been again painting before I came to town for the last couple of weeks. Was going to bring what I've finished, one oil, along to show you but didn't, just as well now that I find you still in the country. You will see it next time I come over. I think you will like it. It's quite American, I think—no one will want it."[47]

One of the last of his major works based on Lancaster architecture was produced in 1931. Demuth wrote to Stieglitz in September, and his comments reveal what his life was like at this point: "My summer, well it's almost over and as I realize this fact I also realize that most of it found me numb. I've gardened and I've sun-burned myself, and maybe I've painted. I think, really, my summer's painting, only one, is all right. I think that you will like it, too. It's an oil and seems more to the point than most, different I feel, perhaps I'm just, in my suffering, making myself feel this, from my others. Anyway it has a grand name, it's called: 'And in the Land of the Brave.'"[48] The painting, *"And the Home of the Brave"* (The Art Institute of Chicago, Farnham 1959, painting no. 551) was based on buildings in Lancaster, with a title borrowed from the national anthem.

Demuth was more fortunate than many of his artist contemporaries. Although he was never rich, his living circumstances were comfortable throughout his career, and he had fewer financial problems than many of the artists who were his friends. His work always sold moderately well. Demuth's still lifes were among the most popular of his works, though the consequences of this were sometimes frustrating to the artist: "Some one in Boston must have a drawing, it seems, of that vintage,—the result of McBride chez 'Creative Art,' you know.—'If there was only an acrobat drawing I'd take that.' And if there was an acrobat drawing they'd want peaches. What most of them really need is a bananna [sic]."[49] Demuth enjoyed a comparatively favorable reception from the critics, although they often read too much into the works: "How beautiful and how terrible the flowers: daisies with cabalistic secrets, cyclamens rosy with vice, orchids wet with the mystery of the Rosicru-cians!"[50] Or, "Demuth's flowers move in the Proustian world of suggestibility and infinite adumbrations."[51]

Those who had admired his watercolors of flowers and fruit were disappointed in the twenties when he produced fewer of them, as an anonymous reviewer lamented in 1926: "All that has gone, and we must be content to accept something else in its place, something infinitely less gracious, hard, and rather metallic."[52] Demuth's sales never equaled his critical reputation, as Stieglitz complained to him in 1930: "Several people have been after your 'Green Pears,' but balked at $2500.00 saying that at Kraushaar's, etc., etc.—Always the same old story.—They concede the particular picture to be finer than any one 'there'—but—yes, ye gods—but!—I seem always to be in the position of money-gouger—most amusing when in all the years of gouging I have yet to receive a penny from the gouging!—And none of the artists I have gouged for have become rich like the French artists so lovingly supported by art loving America!"[53]

Despite the relatively greater appreciation of his work compared to that of some of his contemporaries, support for modern art in America was still not widespread, and Demuth felt keenly the lack of a wider American audience. By the mid-1920s, many American artists had begun to feel as he did: "I wish that some 'movie star' or, whatever, would make the art of the United States fashionable. Appreciation is too much to hope for,—but, at times I think we may see it (our art) become fashionable in our time. That would help,—or, you know; would be in one way 'appre-ciation.'"[54] Demuth was fortunate to live to witness increasing acclaim for his art. A. E. Gallatin devoted several pages to Demuth in his *American Water-Colourists* in 1922 and wrote a monograph on him, the first major publication on the artist's work, which appeared in 1927.

Demuth's last works were a series of watercolors of the beach at Provincetown, where he spent the late summer and early fall of 1934. He had always enjoyed Provincetown, but this was his first visit since 1930, when he and Darrell Larsen also visited Jack and Blanche Steinman of Lancaster on Nantucket. These late works (see no. 38) abandon the architectonic rigidity of his temperas of buildings, as well as the carefully structured character of his still lifes. The figures consist of a few penciled lines, given form as colors floating against the bright sand. In the year following that summer the artist did not paint again.

Charles Demuth died of diabetes on October 23, 1935, in Lancaster at the age of fifty-two and was buried in the Lancaster Cemetery near his father's grave. His death was a great loss to his friends, who regarded him with enormous affection. Marsden Hartley was moved to write a touching tribute to his colleague entitled "Farewell Charles," in which he reflected, "Charles has only just gone, rest his winsome bones."[55]

In his will, Demuth left his watercolors to Robert Locher, all his other paintings to Georgia O'Keeffe, and almost everything else to his mother. However, when she died in 1943, she remembered many of Demuth's closest friends in her will, leaving the family home to Robert Locher and smaller bequests to others, including the Stettheimer sisters, Henry McBride, and Albert Barnes. After her death, a small auction of a selection of undesignated items was held locally and many Lancastrians were able to acquire Demuth memorabilia.

After he inherited the house, Robert Locher and his friend Richard C. Weyand turned the first floor of the Demuth home into a shop, from which they sold gifts, antiques, and occasionally a Demuth work, mostly to Lancaster residents. Weyand made a catalogue of works by Demuth and a scrapbook of articles concerning the artist. When Locher died in 1956, he bequeathed everything to Weyand. Unfortunately, Weyand died only three months later without a will, and many important archival materials that Weyand originally had intended to leave to Yale University were dispersed among several of his relatives. Some smaller works and memorabilia were disposed of in Lancaster, but more important paintings and drawings were sold at auction at Parke-Bernet Galleries in New York in two extensive sales in 1957 and 1958, which contained the greatest number of works by Demuth ever offered to the public.

After the artist's death, several exhibitions of his work were assembled, including a memorial exhibition at the Whitney Museum of American Art in New York, which opened late in 1937[56] and a retrospective held at the Museum of Modern Art in 1950.[57] Lancastrians, too, were finally able to view a formal presentation of his work locally when two small exhibitions were mounted at the Fackenthal Library, Franklin and Marshall College, one in 1941[58] and the other in 1948.[59]

Since that time, Demuth's artistic reputation has steadily grown. As American avant-garde art of his period has received increasing attention, the interpretation of the career and work of artists like Demuth has become more sophisticated as scholars investigate the influences that have shaped an artist. In Charles Demuth's case, Paris and New York were vital to developing his aesthetic principles, but it was in Lancaster that his artistic sensibilities were nurtured and achieved fruition.

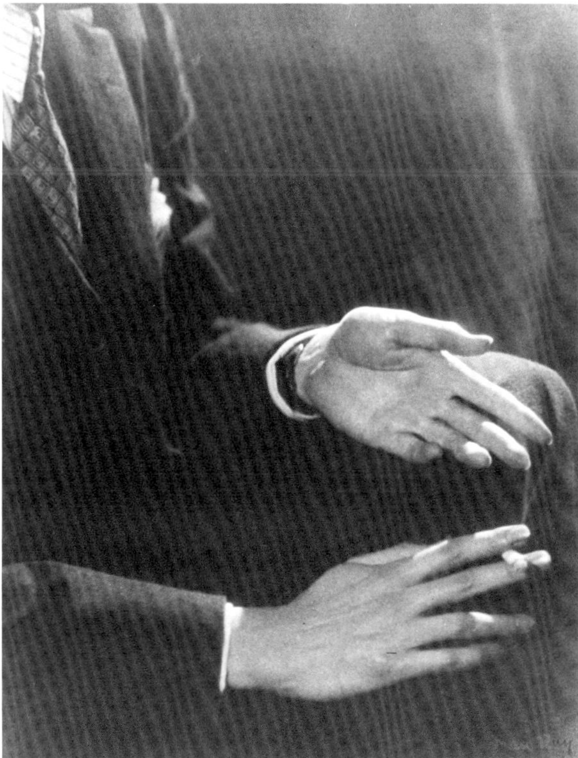

Fig. 6. Hands of Charles Demuth, by Man Ray, c. 1921 (Paul M. Hertzmann, Inc.)

Notes

1. *The Little Review*, vol. 12, no. 2 (May 1929), pp. 30–31.

2. McBride 1938, p. 22.

3. Hartley 1936, p. 559.

4. Soby 1944, p. 9.

5. Wellman 1931, p. 484.

6. Farnham 1959, p. 952.

7. Demuth to Stieglitz, June 4, 1928 (Yale University).

8. Farnham 1959, p. 981.

9. The phrase was a favorite of his: "My Christmas was quiet in the province" (Demuth to Shane, Agnes, and Eugene O'Neill, December 1919[?] (Yale University); "Well, you must come to see us in the province" (Demuth to Eugene and Agnes O'Neill, 1926[?] (Yale University); and "Hoping to see you before I go back to my province" (Demuth to Selma Kenkig, Archives, Philadelphia Museum of Art).

10. Helen Henderson, "Art and Artists Pass in Review," *Philadelphia Inquirer*, December 1, 1918.

11. Demuth to Alfred Stieglitz, October 12, 1926 (Yale University).

12. *See* Demuth 1925. Tobacco was a leading industry of Lancaster County. The business was founded by Christopher Demuth in 1770, and he ran it until 1814. It passed to his son Jacob Demuth, who oversaw the business until 1842. Then it passed to Jacob's three sons, Emmanuel E. Demuth, who ran it in 1842–43 and from 1853 to 1864, Lawrence Demuth, who ran it from 1843 to 1853, and Henry C. Demuth, from 1864 to 1906. At the latter's death, both his sons took it over; Ferdinand A. Demuth, Charles Demuth's father, ran it from 1906, and at Ferdinand's death in 1911, Henry C. Demuth took sole control, running the business until his own death in 1937. His son Christopher Demuth ran it between 1937 and 1978, at which time it was taken over by his widow, Dorothea Demuth, who continues to operate it.

13. *See* Ritchie 1950. A watercolor by Louisa Demuth is reproduced on p. 8 and one by Caroline Demuth on p. 9.

14. Demuth 1912.

15. Farnham 1959, p. 963.

16. Hartley 1936, p. 559.

17. Hartley 1936, p. 560.

18. Henry McBride, "Demuth Phantoms from Literature," *Art News*, vol. 49, no. 1 (March 1950), p. 20.

19. Williams 1951, p. 151.

20. Williams to Marianne Moore, August 23, 1928, in John C. Thirwell, *The Selected Letters of William Carlos Williams* (New York, 1957), p. 107.

21. Henry McBride, review, *New York Sun*, November 1, 1914.

22. George Biddle, *An American Artist's Story* (Boston, 1939), p. 216.

23. Gallatin 1927, p. 3.

24. Henry McBride, "Demuth," *New York Sun*, April 10, 1926.

25. Willard Huntington Wright, "The New Painting and American Snobbery," *Arts and Decoration*, vol. 7 (January 1917), p. 152.

26. Demuth to Stieglitz, August 13, 1921 (Yale University).

27. Demuth to Stieglitz, November 28, 1921 (Yale University).

28. Demuth to Stieglitz, October 10, 1921 (Yale University).

29. McBride 1938, p. 23.

30. Gallatin 1927, pp. 7–8.

31. Demuth to Stieglitz, September 4, 1923 (Yale University).

32. Brown 1955, p. 115.

33. "Random Impressions in Current Exhibitions," *New York Tribune*, December 24, 1922. The author was probably Royal Cortissoz, art critic for the paper at the time.

34. Smith 1955, pp. 29 and 73.

35. Henry McBride, "News and Reviews: Charles Demuth Displays His Beautiful Landscapes at Daniel's," *New York Sun*, December 5, 1920.

36. McBride 1923, p. 218.

37. Edward Alden Jewell, "Demuth at the Whitney," *New York Times*, December 19, 1937.

38. Faison 1950, p. 123.

39. These artists have also been described variously as Cubist-Realists (*see* Brown 1943–45, pp. 146–48, 159–60) and as the Immaculates.

40. Stewart 1981, pp. 9–11.

41. Gallatin 1922, p. 23.

42. Stewart 1981, p. 142.

43. Hartley 1936, p. 560.

44. *See* Demuth to Arensberg, n.d., Arensberg Archive, Philadelphia Museum of Art. I am grateful to Anne d'Harnoncourt for bringing this letter to my attention.

45. Soby 1944, p. 10.

46. Watson 1923, p. 338.

47. Demuth to Stieglitz, October 12, 1930 (Yale University).

48. Demuth to Stieglitz, September 10, 1931 (Yale University).

49. Charles Demuth to Alfred Stieglitz, October 16, 1929 (Yale University).

50. Carl Van Vechten, "Pastiches et Pistaches: Charles Demuth and Florine Stettheimer," *The Reviewer*, vol. 2, no. 4 (February 1922), pp. 269–70.

51. James W. Lane, "Notes from New York," *Apollo*, vol. 27, no. 158 (February 1938), p. 96.

52. "New York Exhibitions: Charles Demuth, Intimate Gallery," *Art News*, vol. 24, no. 27 (April 10, 1926), p. 7.

53. Stieglitz to Demuth, January 28, 1930 (Yale University).

54. Demuth to Alfred Stieglitz, January 16, 1926 (Yale University).

55. Hartley 1936, p. 552.

56. New York, Whitney Museum of American Art, *Charles Demuth Memorial Exhibition*, December 15, 1937–January 16, 1938.

57. Andrew Carnduff Ritchie, *Charles Demuth* (New York, 1950) served as the exhibition catalogue.

58. Lancaster, Pa., Arts Committee, The Junior League of Lancaster, *Memorial Exhibition: Water Colors by Charles Demuth, 1883–1935*, exhibited at the Fackenthal Library, Franklin and Marshall College, January 20–26, 1941.

59. Lancaster, Pa., Lancaster County Historical Society and the Fackenthal Library, Franklin and Marshall College, *Twenty-Nine Watercolors by Charles Demuth*, exhibited at the Fackenthal Library, January 3–11, 1948.

Catalogue of the
Exhibition

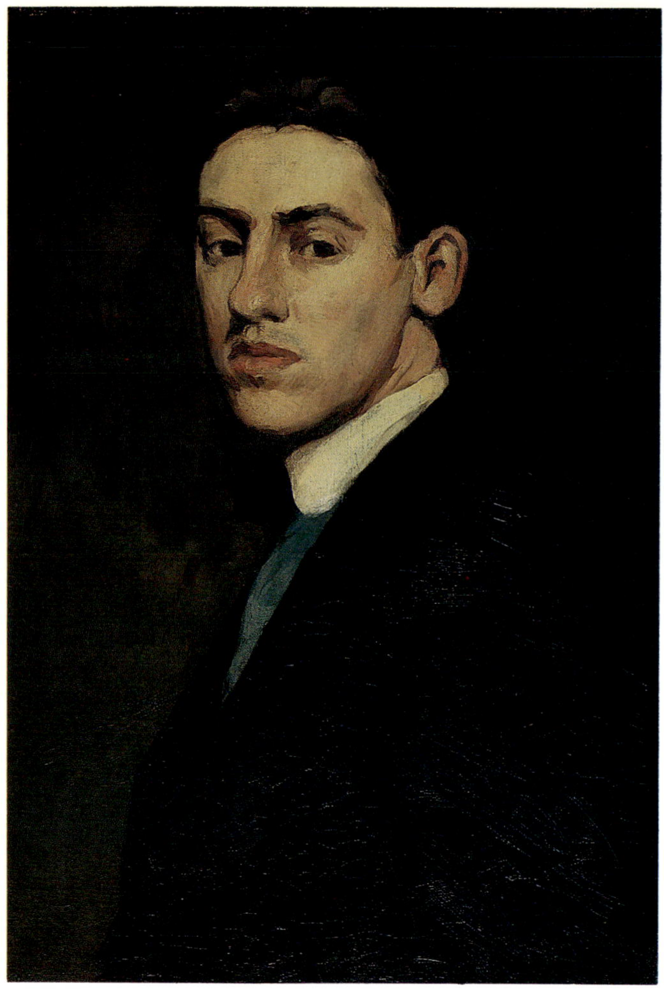

1. Self-Portrait, 1907
Oil on canvas, 26 1/16 x 18"
(66.2 x 45.7 cm)

Private Collection,
Lancaster, Pennsylvania

Farnham 1959, painting
no. 2; Eiseman, no. 8.1907

Provenance: Augusta B.
Demuth, Lancaster; Robert
Locher, Lancaster, 1943;
Richard Weyand, Lancaster,
1956; Margaret Dana,
Lancaster, 1956; private
collection, 1958

One of the earliest surviving works by Charles Demuth, this darkly toned painting is the only true self-portrait of the artist extant, although Demuth occasionally included himself in group scenes, such as *At "The Golden Swan," Sometimes Called "Hell Hole"* (no. 12) and *Turkish Bath,* 1918 (Farnham 1959, painting no. 342). Dating from his student years in Philadelphia, the painting is earthy in color with visible brushstrokes, showing his early style. Its straightforward realism can be compared to the work of Philadelphia artist Thomas Eakins, and its dark, painterly quality to that of Demuth's older contemporaries John Sloan, William Glackens, or Robert Henri, active in Philadelphia and New York and later members of the group of avant-garde painters in New York known as The Eight. No hint of the artist's later flowing, transparent washes or bright, sharply defined colors appears here.

The portrait was included in an exhibition sponsored by two local organizations (Lancaster, Pa., The Iris Club and the Lancaster County Historical Society, *Loan Exhibition of Historical and Contemporary Portraits Illustrating the Evolution of Portraiture in Lancaster County, Pennsylvania* [November 23–December 13, 1912], no 55). This was apparently the only exhibition in Lancaster in which Demuth participated. The Woolworth Building, in which it was held, opened in 1879 at 117 North Queen Street and was the first successful Woolworth store in the United States.

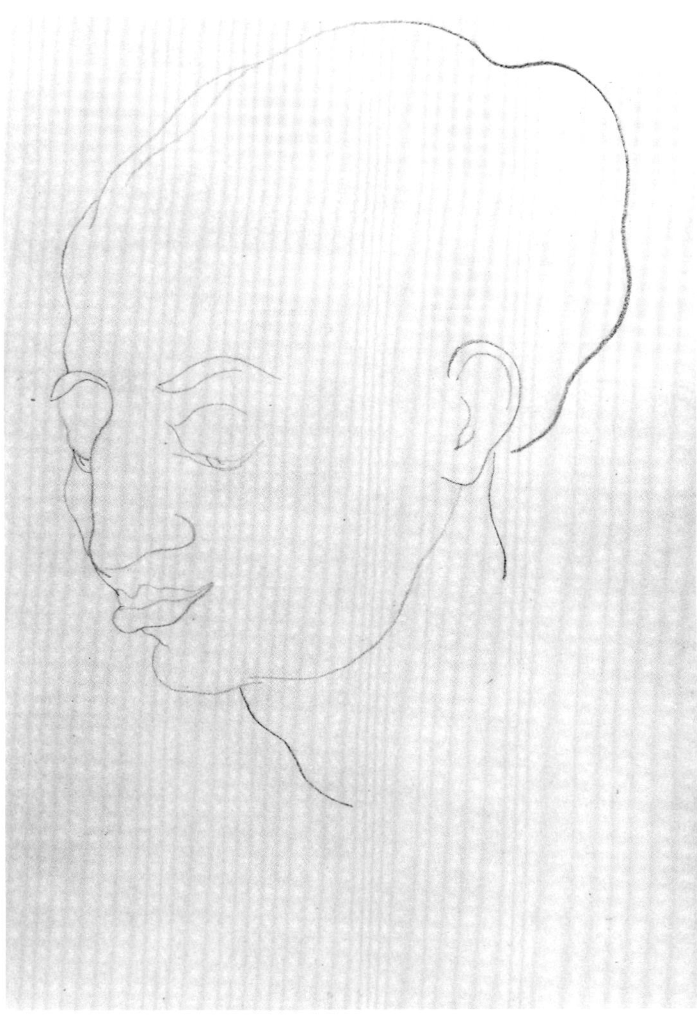

2. Orchestra Conductor #2, c. 1915
Pencil on paper, 10½ x 7³⁄₁₆"
(26.7 x 18.3 cm)

Inscribed, verso, by Robert Locher: drawing by Charles Demuth c. 1915. Willed to Robert E. Locher 193[5]

Private Collection, Lancaster, Pennsylvania

Farnham 1959, drawing no. 178; Eiseman, no. 58.1915

Provenance: Robert Locher, Lancaster, 1935; Edith Allport, 1955; private collection, 1958

This drawing traditionally has been considered a portrait of Leopold Stokowski (1882–1977), who was conductor of the Philadelphia Orchestra from 1912 to 1936. Although Demuth is not known to have met Stokowski, his proximity to Philadelphia would have made him well aware of the conductor's accomplishments, and the resemblance is sufficiently striking to make the identification likely, if not definite.

In its economy of line this drawing is reminiscent of the work of Henri Matisse and Auguste Rodin, which was first shown in America at Alfred Stieglitz's gallery "291" in 1908. Although Demuth frequently employed a combination of pencil and wash, in this particular sheet he succeeded in conveying the effect of volume using only a pencil outline. Critic Henry McBride admired such drawings, but realized that it would be some time before the public would appreciate them: "Officialdom in America doesn't yet know what calligraphic draftsmanship is and consequently is bound to disapprove of it for at least ten years to come" (Henry McBride, "Demuth Memorial Exhibition," *New York Sun*, December 18, 1937. Two similar versions of this drawing are known. One appeared at auction in 1976 (Sotheby Parke Bernet, New York, sale no. 3913, October 28, 1976, lot 24). Another was recorded by Farnham (1959, drawing no. 177) and was formerly in the collection of Mr. and Mrs. C. William Coventry of Lancaster.

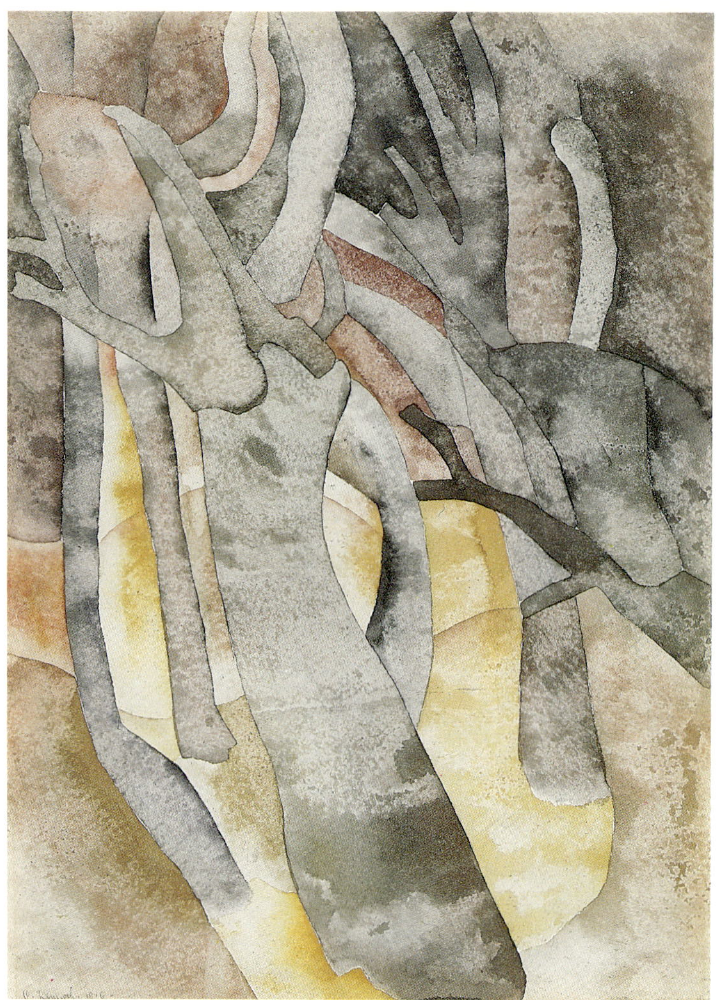

3. Tree Trunks, 1916
Verso: *Abstract Landscape after Marin,* c. 1912–15
(Farnham 1959, painting no. 601)

Watercolor and pencil on paper, 14½ x 10¼"
(36.8 x 26 cm)

Signed, lower left:
C. Demuth—1916—

Collection of
Richard York Gallery,
New York

Farnham 1959, painting no. 715; Eiseman, no. 25.1916

Provenance: Robert Locher, Lancaster, 1935; Richard Weyand, Lancaster, 1956; Herbert S. Levy, Lancaster; Sotheby Parke Bernet, New York, sale no. 4628M, May 29, 1981, lot 89; Richard York Gallery, 1981

Herbert Levy, who once owned this watercolor, was an individual with longstanding Lancaster connections. He attended Franklin and Marshall College in Lancaster and subsequently established his law practice there. After Richard Weyand's death in 1956, Levy served as executor of the estate. He acquired almost a dozen works by Demuth and wrote the article "Charles Demuth of Lancaster" (Levy 1964).

The trees depicted here have been transformed into an abstract pattern, highlighted by deep pinks and yellows. The shapes float against a mottled background, flattened, layered, and reduced to their essential formal elements. However, the forms are still recognizable, for Demuth rarely painted totally abstractly, preferring to retain some connection to the object. Demuth found one of the keys to his mature style in the use of watercolor; his friend Marsden Hartley observed several years later that "his gifts for expression have been evolved almost entirely through this medium" (Hartley 1921, p. 101).

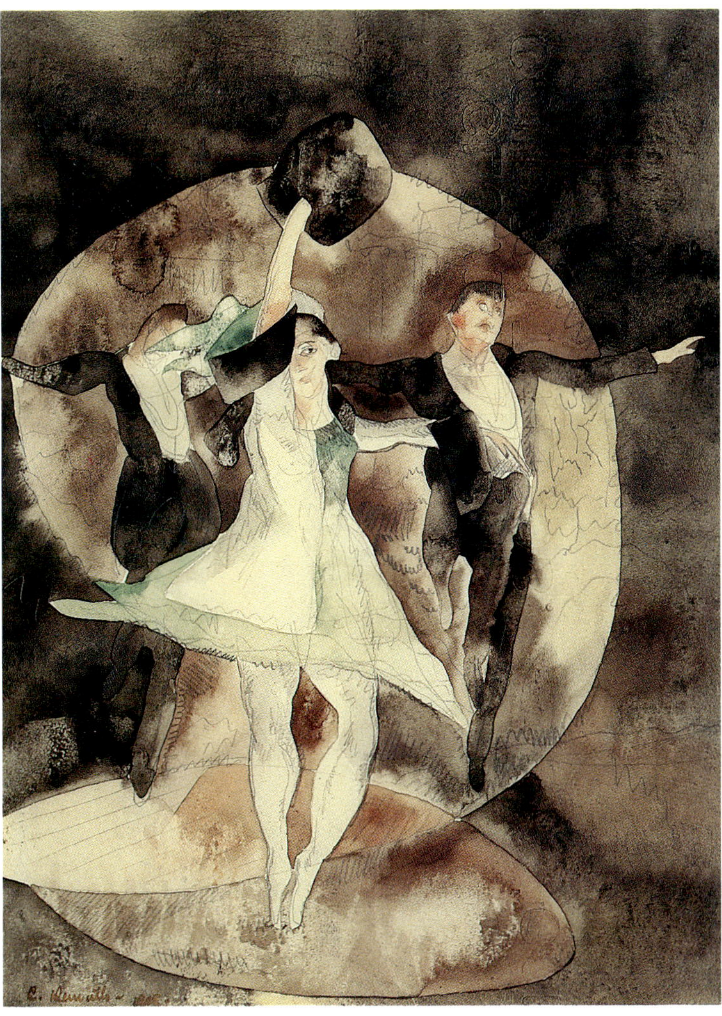

4. In Vaudeville: The Green Dancer, 1916
Watercolor and pencil on paper, 10⅞ x 8″ (27.6 x 20.3 cm)

Signed, lower left: C. Demuth. 1916

Philadelphia Museum of Art. The Samuel S. White, 3rd, and Vera White Collection. 67-30-21

Farnham 1959, painting no. 179; Eiseman, no. 108.1916

Provenance: Earl Horter, Philadelphia; Daniel Gallery, New York; Samuel S. White, 3rd, and Vera White, Ardmore, Pennsylvania; Philadelphia Museum of Art, 1967

Demuth saw vaudeville acts in New York, but many of the watercolors he executed on this theme were based on revues he saw in Lancaster, either at the Colonial Theatre or at the Fulton Opera House, both near his home. He was especially fascinated by the dancers, whose seemingly boneless anatomies he captured in this watercolor. Demuth's friend Marsden Hartley also admired vaudeville dancers: "We have been given much, of late, of that virtuosity of foot and leg which is usually called dancing; and that is excellent among us here, quite the contribution of the American, so singularly the product of this special physique. Sometimes I think there are no other dancers but Americans. It used to be so delightful a diversion watching our acrobat and his group with their strong and graceful bodies writhing with rhythmical certitude over a bar or upon a trapeze against a happily colored space" (Hartley 1921, pp. 155–56).

Vera and Samuel S. White, 3rd, became close friends with Demuth and the artist bequeathed to them one of his most prized possessions, a watercolor by John Marin. The Whites were especially important as collectors of modern art, and their artist friends, from whom they also acquired works of art, included Rodin, Matisse, Jules Pascin, and Marin, as well as Demuth and the Philadelphia modernists Arthur B. Carles and Earl Horter. They were also acquainted with another important patron of modern art, Dr. Albert C. Barnes, who shared a taste for Demuth's work. Their collection contained some nine watercolors by him, bought during the artist's lifetime as well as after his death (See "The Samuel S. White, 3rd, and Vera White Collection," Philadelphia Museum of Art, *Bulletin,* vol. 63, nos. 296–97 [January–March and April–June 1968].)

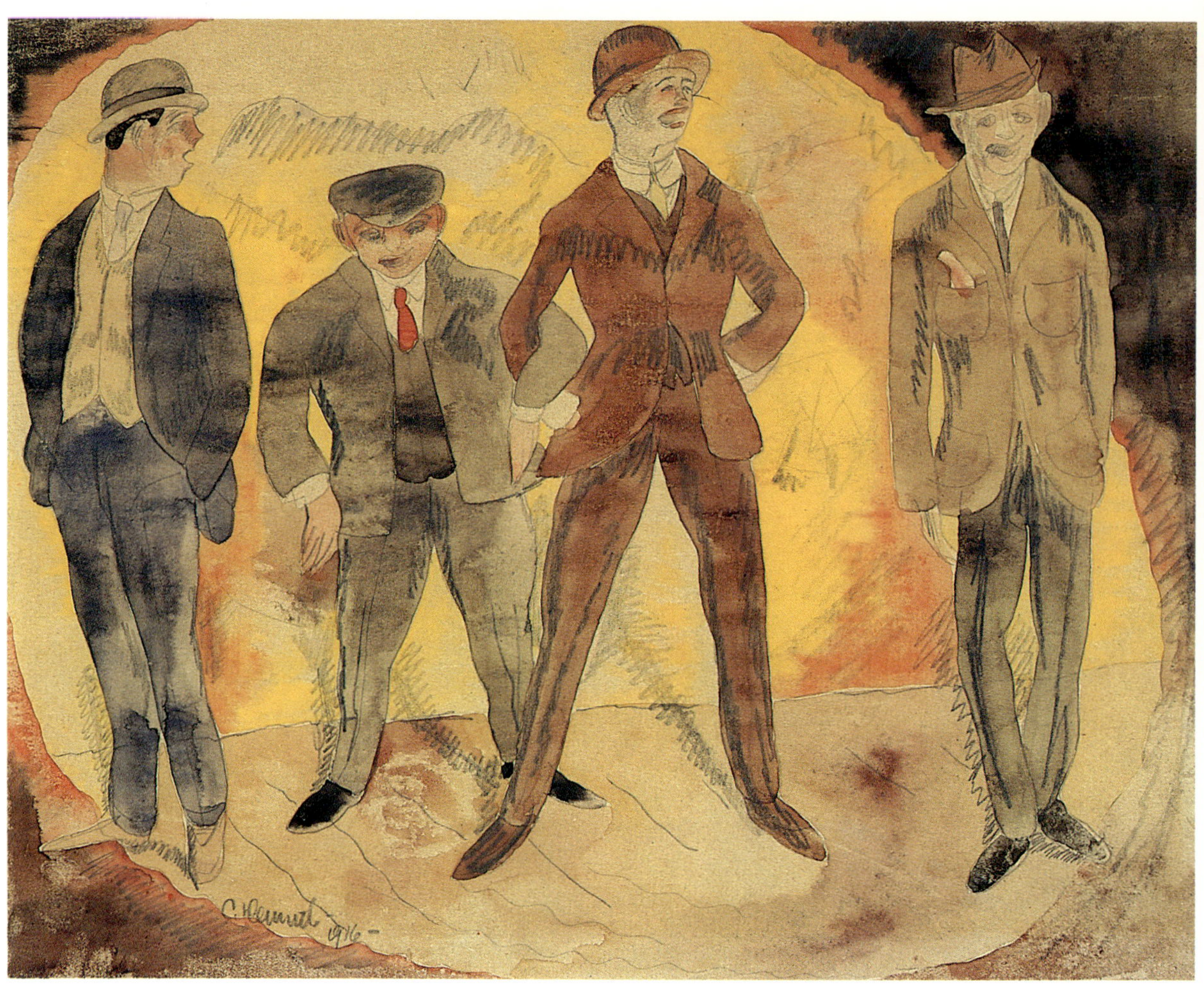

**5. In Vaudeville:
Barbershop Quartet,**
1916
Watercolor and pencil
on paper, 8¾ x 11"
(22.2 x 27.9 cm)

Signed and inscribed,
lower left: C. Demuth—
/1916—

Mr. and Mrs. R. Meyer de
Schauensee, Devon,
Pennsylvania

Provenance: Carlen
Gallery, Philadelphia;
Mr. and Mrs. R. Meyer de
Schauensee, 1946 or 1947

Shown only in Philadelphia

A lurid yellow and orange background
enlivens the composition and effectively
conveys the effect of bright stage lights on the
four performers. This barbershop quartet was
undoubtedly preceded or followed on stage by
acrobats, dancers, and other singers, who
made up the wide variety of vaudeville
entertainment, which fascinated Demuth.

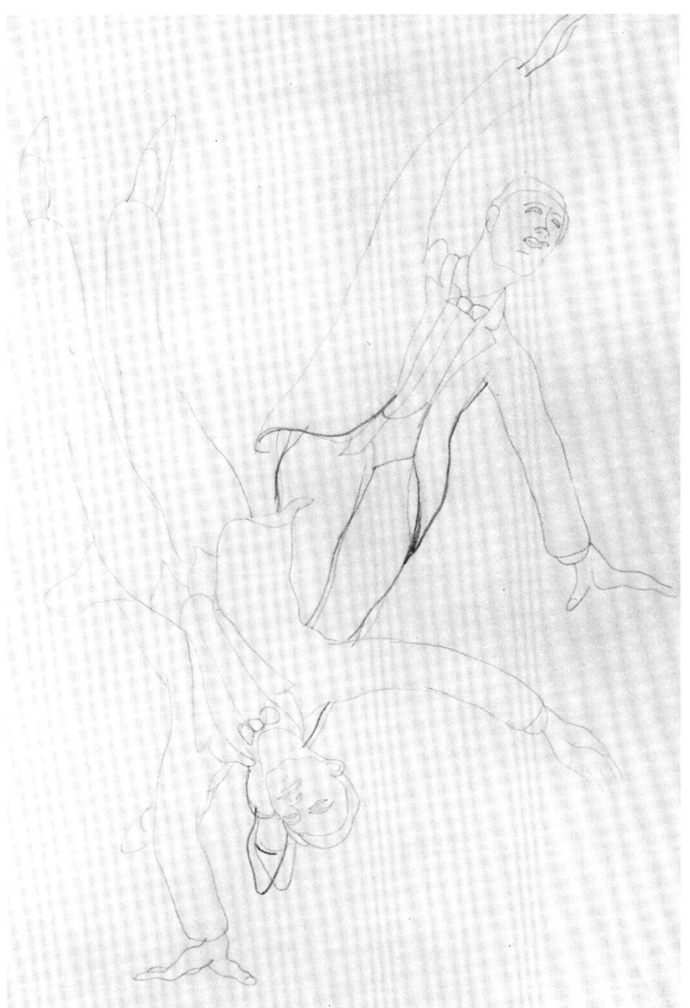

6. In Vaudeville: Acrobats, 1918
Pencil on paper, 12⅞ x 8½"
(32.7 x 21.6 cm)

Inscribed, verso, by Robert
Locher: Preliminary line
drawing for watercolor
"Two Acrobats"/by
Charles Demuth, 1916/
willed to Robert E. Locher, /
1935

Private Collection,
Lancaster, Pennsylvania

Farnham 1959, drawing no.
6; Eiseman, no. 40.1918

Provenance: Robert Locher,
Lancaster, 1935; private
collection, c. 1949

Demuth surely would have agreed with the sentiments of his friend Marsden Hartley, who regretted the passing of vaudeville entertainments such as these acrobats: "Where is our once charming acrobat—our minstrel of muscular music? What has become of these groups of fascinating people gotten up in silk and spangle? Who may the evil genius be who has taken them and their fascinating art from our stage, who the ogre of taste that has dispensed with them and their charm? How seldom it is in these times that one encounters them, as formerly when they were so much the charming part of our lighter entertainment. What are they doing since popular and fickle notions have removed them from our midst?" (Hartley 1921, p. 155).

Acrobats were a favorite vaudeville theme for Demuth, and his energetic yet sure line was especially suited to this subject; as one critic noted, "the performers [are] just as wobbly in the picture as they are quite intentionally on the stage" (William Stanley Hall, *Eyes on America: The United States as Seen by Her Artists* [New York, 1939], p. 94). The lack of a ground line makes the performers appear to float as they present their routine with effortless elegance. Demuth used the same composition for several works (see Ritchie 1950, p. 30; Sotheby Parke Bernet, sale no. 3913, October 28, 1976, lot 21; Sotheby Parke Bernet, sale no. 4628M, May 29, 1981, lot 96). Contrary to Robert Locher's inscription dating this particular drawing 1916, Alvord Eiseman believes that all the variations were actually produced in 1918, the date that Demuth himself inscribed on a watercolor version, *In Vaudeville: Two Acrobats #1* (Walker Art Center, Minneapolis; Farnham 1959, painting no. 322).

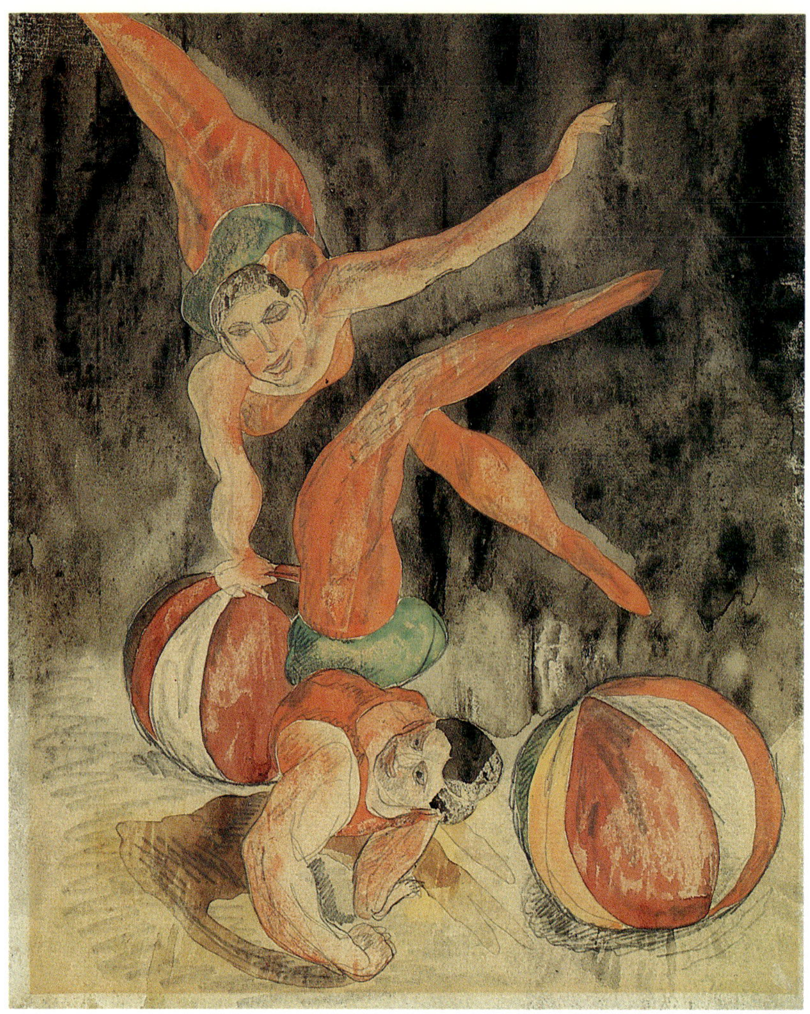

In this watercolor, Demuth is typically more concerned with recreating a visual impression of the actual performance than with accurately delineating the figures' anatomies. The acrobats' positions are physically impossible, yet the artist effectively evokes their fluid movements and seemingly effortless tumbling. The contrast of vivid costumes against a black background accentuates the lively arabesques of curving legs and arms, further intensified with pencil shading. These acrobats possess that "muscular virtuosity" and "poetry of the body" that caused Marsden Hartley to term such performances "a really worthy kind of expression"; as the acrobat came to play a diminishing role in vaudeville entertainments, Hartley expressed his nostalgia for the "elongated and elastic gentlemen" (Hartley 1921, pp. 156–61).

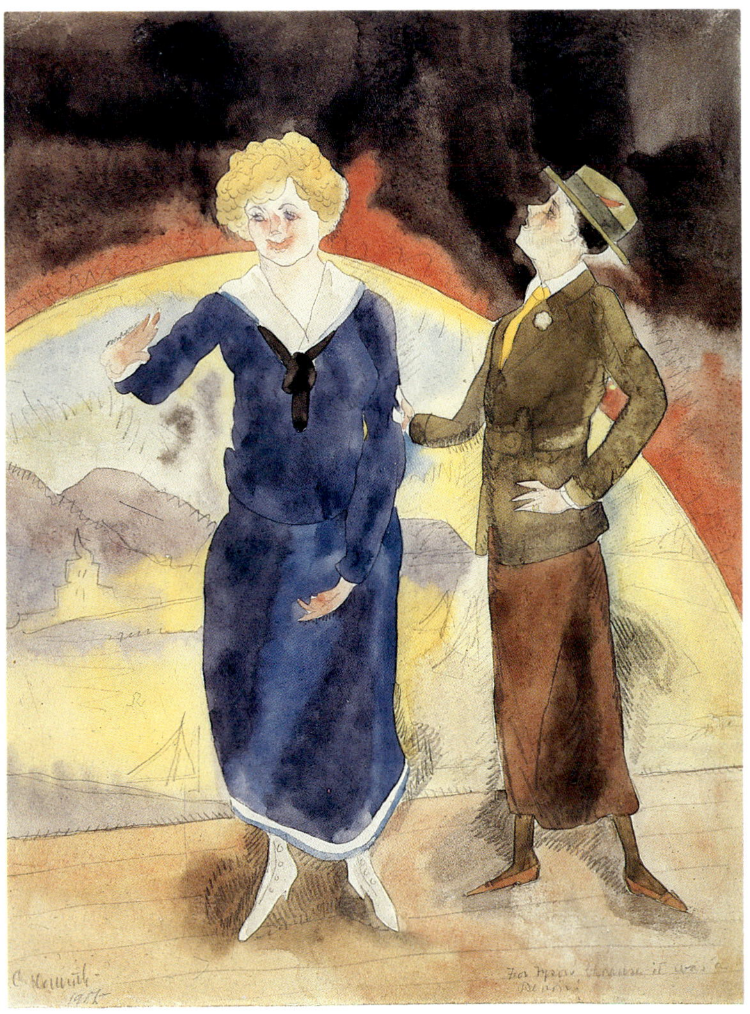

**3. In Vaudeville:
Comediennes,** 1917
Watercolor and pencil on
paper, 10⅝ x 9"
(27 x 22.9 cm)

Signed, lower left:
C. Demuth—1917—;
inscribed, lower right: For
Tyson because it was a/
Renoir!

Private Collection,
Gladwyne, Pennsylvania

Provenance: Carroll S.
Tyson, Philadelphia; private
collection

Two women perform on a wooden stage
against a brightly colored background of red,
yellow, and lavender. It is likely that this is a
comedy routine, since the sprightly gestures of
the two figures convey a humorous situation.
Demuth's impressions are recorded here using
his customary technique of adept pencil
sketches overlaid with watercolor washes. The
work's inscription, to Carroll S. Tyson
(1878–1956), refers to Tyson's particular fond-
ness for Renoir. Tyson owned one of Philadelphia's finest collections and was himself a
distinguished painter in the late Impressionist
style. His superb works by Cézanne, Renoir,
Manet, van Gogh, and Degas were given to
the Philadelphia Museum of Art in 1963. *See*
John Rewald, "The Collection of Carroll S.
Tyson, Jr., Philadelphia, U.S.A.," *The
Connoisseur*, vol. 134 (August 1954), pp. 62–70;
reprinted in Philadelphia Museum of Art,
Bulletin, vol. 59, no. 280 (winter 1964).

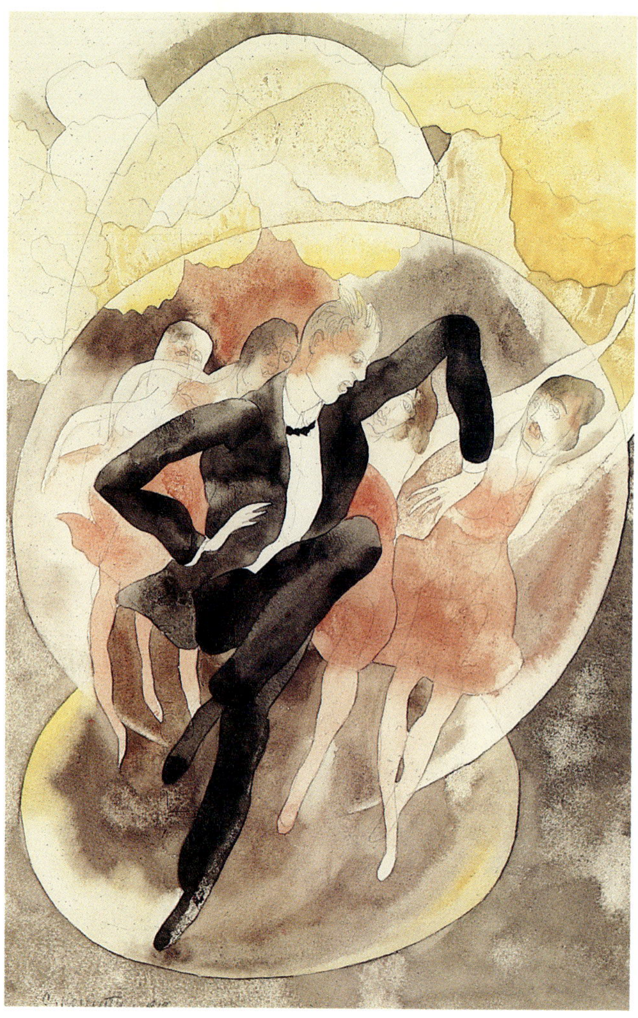

9. In Vaudeville: Dancer with Chorus,
1918
Watercolor and pencil on paper, 13 x 8⅛"
(33 x 20.6 cm)

Signed, lower left:
C. Demuth. 1918—

Philadelphia Museum of Art. A.E. Gallatin Collection. 52-61-18

Farnham 1959, painting no. 321; Eiseman, no. 32.1918

Provenance: Albert E. Gallatin, New York, by 1929; Philadelphia Museum of Art, 1952

Demuth's watercolor technique was particularly suitable for vaudeville scenes, for it enabled him to capture the fast-moving spectacle. So artful were the movement and color that Marsden Hartley wrote: "I do not know why I think of vaudeville as I think of a collection of good drawings. Unless it is because the sense of form is the same in all of the arts. The acrobat certainly has line and mass to think of, even if that isn't his primal concern. He knows how he decorates the space on which he operates" (Hartley 1921, p. 168). This work was exhibited at the Sesqui-Centennial Exposition in Philadelphia in 1926, where Demuth received a silver medal for his 1925 watercolor *Plums* (Addison Gallery of American Art, Phillips Academy, Andover, Mass., Farnham 1959, painting no. 473).

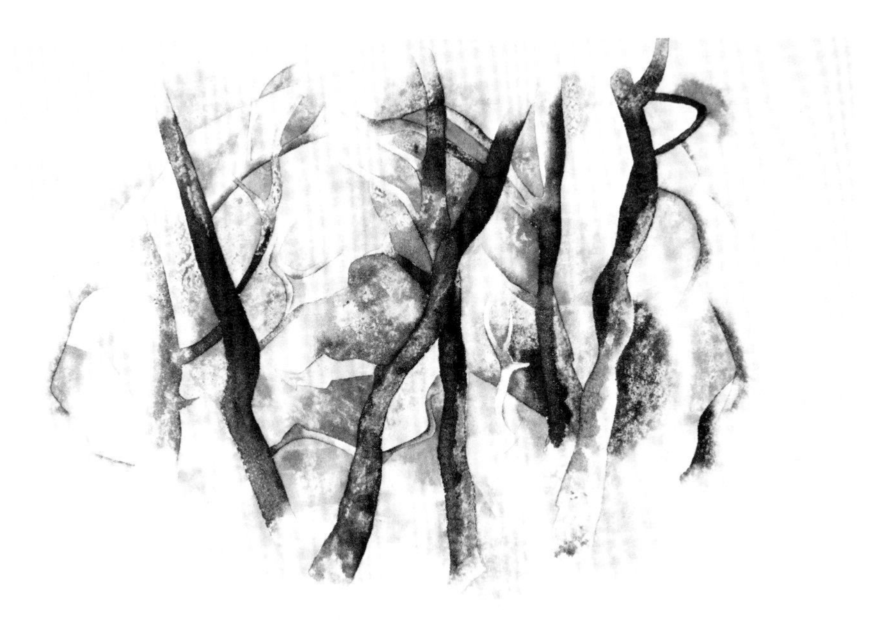

Demuth began his first serious exploration of the visual possibilities of Cubism, which he applied to the study of architecture and landscape, in Bermuda during the winter of 1916–17. He almost certainly knew the structured and analytical landscapes of Cubist precursor Paul Cézanne, shown at Alfred Stieglitz's gallery "291" in 1911, and probably had seen Cubist works in New York or during his trip to Paris in 1912–14. Artist friends like Marsden Hartley, one of Demuth's companions in Bermuda, were well acquainted with modern movements in Europe and also must have been a source of information for him. Demuth applied all of these visual lessons to his studies in Bermuda, where he reduced the forms he saw to carefully drawn planes enlivened by curved forms. In keeping with Cubist coloration, Demuth favored muted tones like the delicate grays and greens used here. Yet works like this appealed to people not usually enthusiastic about modern art, as one critic noted in 1917: "Most of Mr. Demuth's present show is given up to work that is frankly cubistic and you will be astonished, perhaps, to learn that it is being liked, for many people have been going about saying that at last there would be an end of cubism" ("At New York Galleries," *Fine Arts Journal,* vol. 35 [December 1917], pp. 52–53).

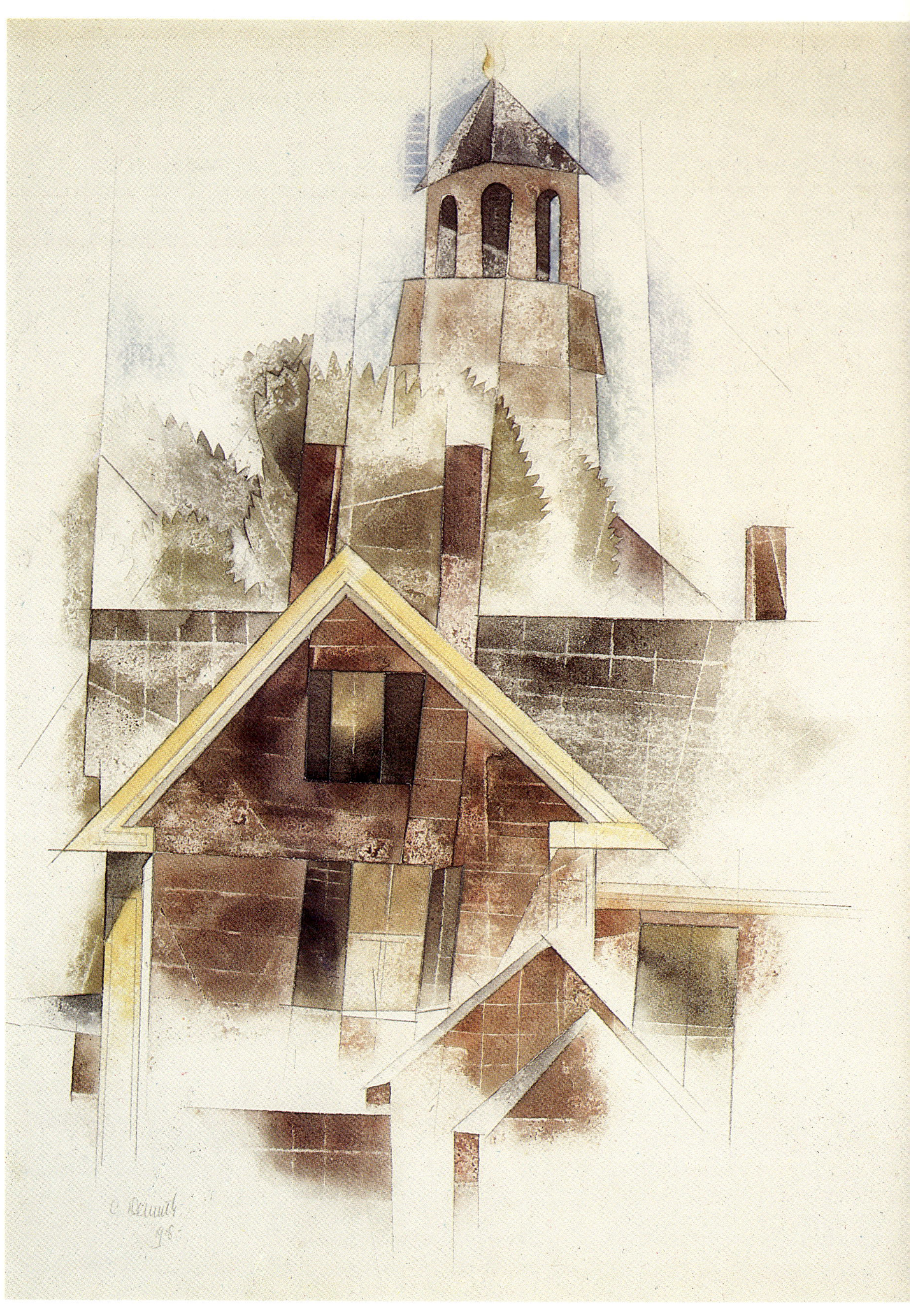

This, the only major work by Demuth that remains in the possession of a relative, was once owned by Charles's cousin Christopher, who ran the family tobacco business from 1937 until his death in 1978.

Demuth had been especially fascinated by the visual possibilities of architecture as a subject for his watercolors since his visit to Bermuda during the winter of 1916–17. Although he had first visited Provincetown, Massachusetts, during the summer of 1914 and had executed a number of works while there, his experimentation in Bermuda and in Gloucester, Massachusetts, inspired him to a new appreciation of the crisp angles of the gables, the clean lines of the clapboard, and the warm bricks of the structures of Provincetown. This watercolor was shown at Stieglitz's Intimate Gallery in 1929 and included in the "Charles Demuth Memorial Exhibition," held at the Whitney Museum of American Art, New York, December 15, 1937—January 16, 1938. It has been exhibited only twice since, at the Fackenthal Library of Franklin and Marshall College, Lancaster, in 1941 and 1948.

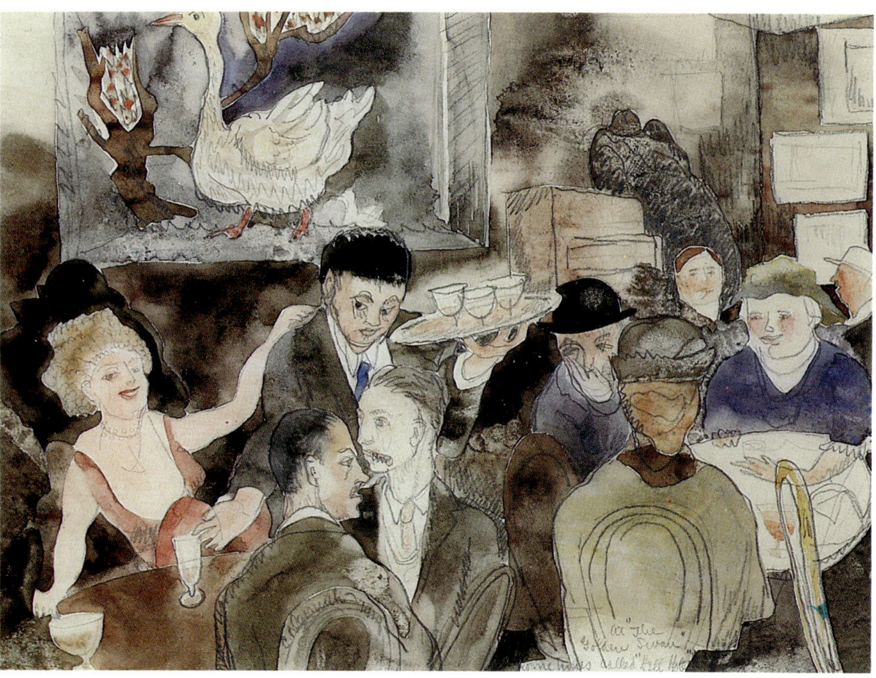

12. At "The Golden Swan," Sometimes Called "Hell Hole,"
1919
Watercolor and pencil on paper, 8 x 10½"
(20.3 x 26.7 cm)

Signed, lower left: C. Demuth 1919; inscribed, lower right: At "The/ Golden Swan"/ sometimes called "Hell Hole"

Collection of Irwin Goldstein, M.D., Wayne, New Jersey

Farnham 1959, painting no. 604; Eiseman, no. 32.1919

Provenance: Robert Locher, Lancaster, 1935; Richard Weyand, Lancaster, 1956; Herbert S. Levy, Lancaster; Sotheby Parke Bernet, New York, sale no. 4628M, May 29, 1981, lot 76; Hirschl & Adler Galleries, New York, 1981; Irwin Goldstein, 1982

The Golden Swan, better known to its clientele by its more vivid nickname, Hell Hole, was in Greenwich Village between Fourth Street and Sixth Avenue. One habitué, John Sloan, recorded the artists' popular gathering spot in the 1917 etching *Hell Hole*, in which he pictured the playwright Eugene O'Neill, who later incorporated some of his experiences there into his plays, including *The Iceman Cometh*. Its "seedily picturesque interior" has been abstracted and borders on caricature while still managing to convey the ambience of the bar: "The Hell Hole was a representative Irish saloon. It had a sawdust covered floor, rude wooden tables, and was filled with the smell of sour beer and mingled sounds of alcoholic woe and laughter. Its barroom was entered from the corner of Sixth Avenue and Fourth Street—the 'front room,' in which women were not allowed. Above the doorway swung a wooden sign decorated with a tarnished gilt swan. Farther east, on Fourth Street, was the 'family entrance,' a glass door that gave access to a small, dank, gaslit chamber known as the 'backroom.' Wooden tables clustered about a smoking potbellied stove, and it was here that respectable Irish widows came to cry into their five-cent mugs of beer" (Arthur and Barbara Gelb, *O'Neill* [New York, 1973], p. 284).

Marcel Duchamp, who had been in the United States since 1915, is depicted seated at the left-hand table to the right of Demuth (who seldom portrayed himself in his work). Duchamp was frequently in Demuth's company during this period, and also appears in Demuth's *The Purple Pup,* 1918 (Museum of Fine Arts, Boston; Farnham 1959, painting no. 246), another Greenwich Village café scene. Duchamp recalled their socializing: "The Hell Hole (the "Golden Swan" in the Village), the Bar[r]on Wilkins (a café) in Harlem, a costumed ball at Webster Hall, Cafés Brevoort and Lafayette were Demuth's favorite places about 1915–16 and he used to take me along. . . . He had a curious smile reflecting an incessant curiosity for every manifestation life offered. An artist worthy of the name, without the pettiness which afflicts most artists; worshipping his inner self without the usual eagerness to be right. Demuth was also one of the few artists whom all other artists liked as a real friend, a rare case indeed. His work is a living illustration of the disappearance of a "Monroe Doctrine" applied to Art; for today, art is no more the crop of privileged soils, and Demuth is among the first to have planted the good seed in America" (Marcel Duchamp, "A Tribute to the Artist," quoted in Ritchie 1950, p. 17).

Such social outings undoubtedly served as a welcome contrast to the more limited possibilities Lancaster offered, and were a source of subjects for his watercolors. Not everyone approved of his night life and the works it inspired: "What excuses young Mr. Duchamp and young Mr. Fisk can offer for descending into such resorts I cannot imagine. They may say they went along to protect Mr. Demuth in the performance of his duty" (Henry McBride, "An Underground Search for Higher Moralities," *New York Sun*, November 25, 1917).

In its fluid lines and flowing watercolor washes, this café scene is close in style to Demuth's illustrations of *Nana* by Emile Zola and *The Turn of the Screw* and "The Beast in the Jungle" by Henry James, which date from the same period.

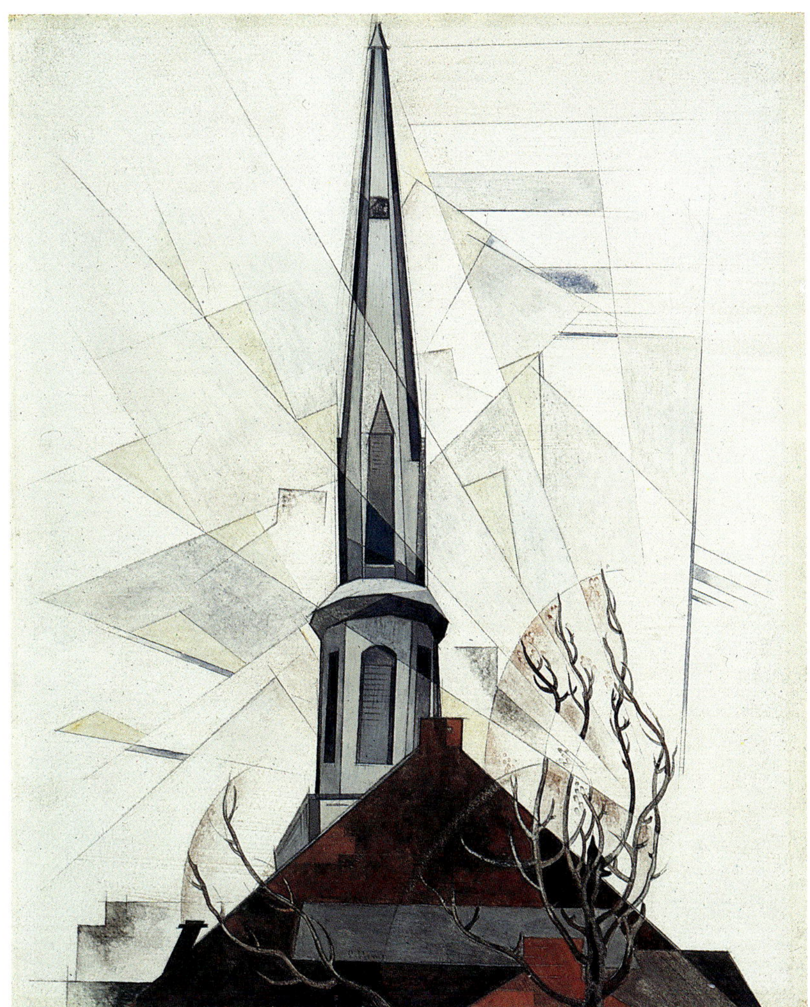

This is one of three paintings bearing the same title; the others date from 1920 (nos. 14 and 16). Although the inclusion of "#7" in the inscription (in Demuth's handwriting) implies that there were four other works with this title, they have not come to light. The title refers to the artist's native Lancaster, which he commonly referred to as "the province" or "my province," and where Saint John's German Reformed Church, depicted here, was located. Razed in 1964, the structure stood at the corner of North Mulberry and West Orange streets (*see* fig. 7). In contrast to the flattened forms of the Boston work, here the slender, pointed spire of the church rising above a dark gable pierces the sky, fragmenting the surface into crisply faceted Cubist planes and dynamic angles that resemble Futurist lines of force, resulting in a visually powerful composition.

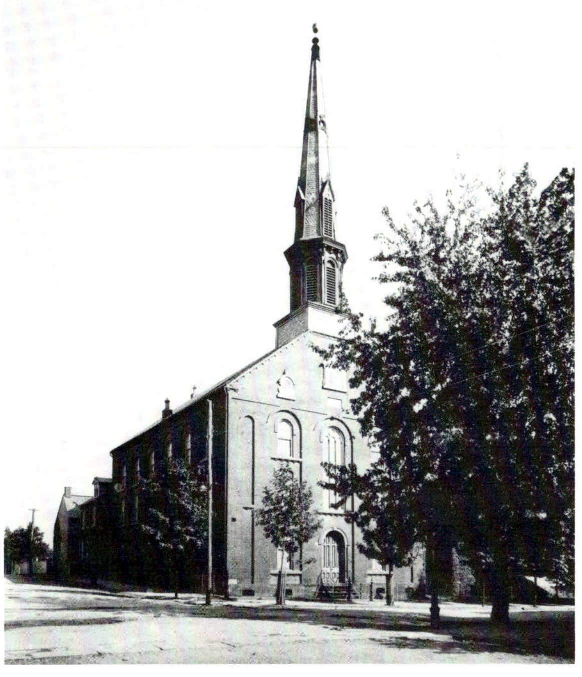

Fig. 7. Saint John's German Reformed Church. Published in *Art Work of Lancaster* (Chicago: W. H. Parish Publishing Co., 1892)

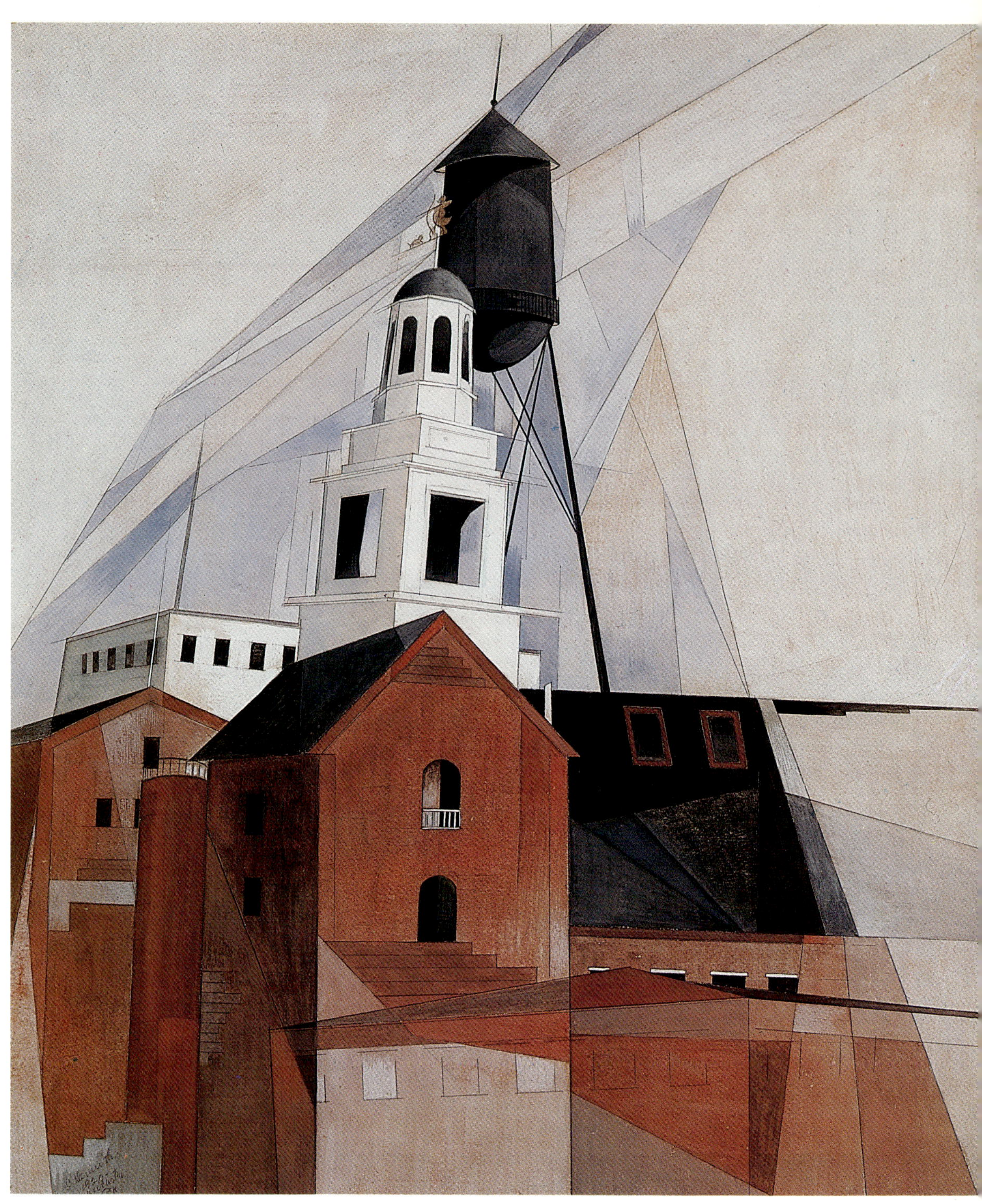

The building depicted in this work still stands in Lancaster on South Prince Street at the corner of Farnum Street, not far from the Demuth house. Formerly the Schroeder-Spencer cotton mill, it was owned by the P. Lorillard Company when Demuth painted it in 1920 (*see* fig. 8). The building is easily recognizable, but Demuth avoided recording it exactly as it was, shifting angles, moving elements closer together, and exaggerating the viewpoint in order to create an image not visible from the street. Even if he had stood in a window of one of the upper stories of the Conestoga Mills directly across from the Lorillard building, the scene would not appear exactly as he painted it. Demuth elongated the forms and placed them against a faceted sky to give the work visual tension and energy. The technique he used here is typical of his architectural pieces, made up of thin layers of precisely applied tempera. *Lancaster* was the sort of work that caused Henry McBride to note that Demuth grew "in strength if not in gaiety" as his artistic interests became more and more absorbed by architectural subjects (McBride 1921, p. 235).

By the time this work was painted, its former owners, the poet and writer Walter Arensberg (1878–1954) and his wife, Louise, had assembled one of the finest collections of modern art in America. The Arensbergs hosted artistic soirees in their apartment on West Sixty-seventh Street in New York between about 1915 and 1920, which were attended by an international group of artists and writers, including Marcel Duchamp, Jean Crotti, Francis Picabia, Albert Gleizes, Man Ray, Charles Sheeler, Morton Schamberg, and Charles Demuth. This circle was instrumental in formulating important avant-garde artistic theories of the day (*see* Francis Naumann, "Walter Conrad Arensberg: Poet, Patron, and Participant in the New York Avant-Garde, 1915–20," Philadelphia Museum of Art, *Bulletin*, vol. 76, no. 328 [spring 1980]). The Arensbergs owned one other work by Demuth, a 1917 watercolor, *Bermuda* (Philadelphia Museum of Art, The Louise and Walter Arensberg Collection, 50-134-44).

Fig. 8. P. Lorillard Company tobacco buildings, c. 1950 (Courtesy of S. Lane Faison, Jr.)

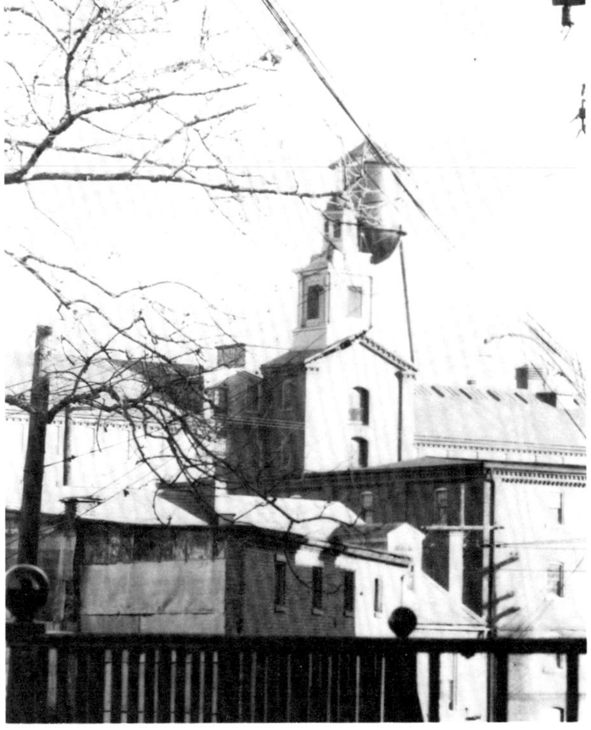

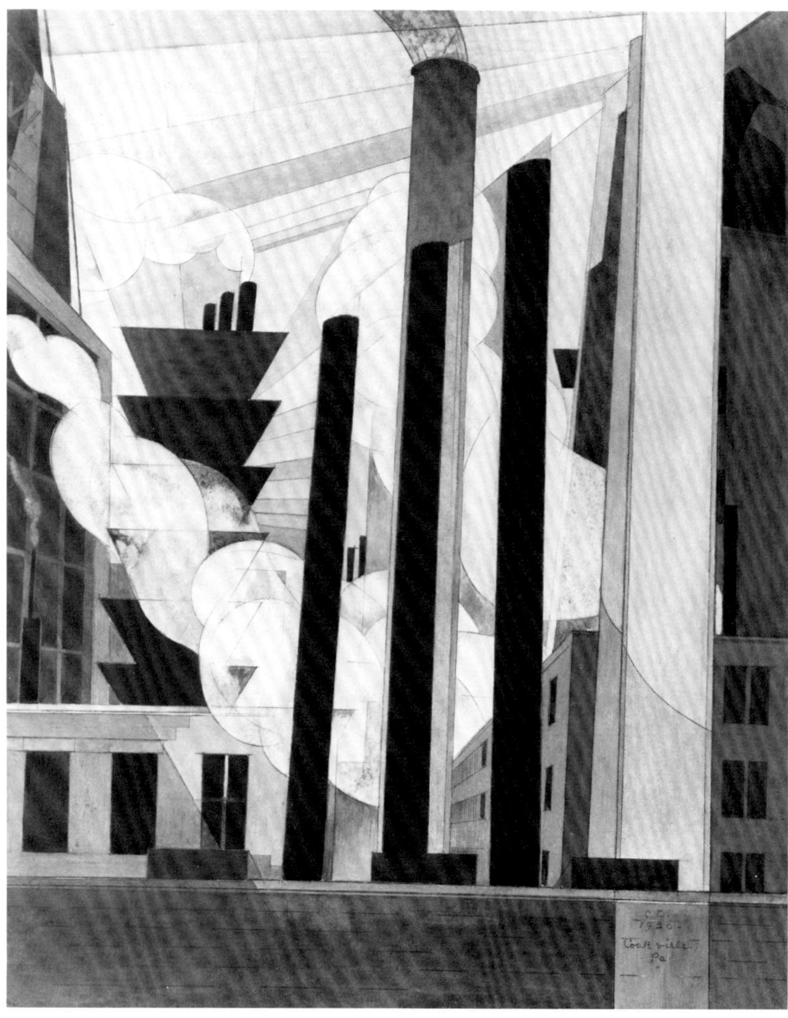

15. End of the Parade: Coatesville, Pa. (The Milltown), 1920
Tempera and pencil on composition board, 19⅞ x 15¾" (50.5 x 40 cm).

Signed and inscribed, lower right: C.D./—1920—/Coatsville [sic], Pa.; verso: "The End of the Parade"/ C. Demuth/1920

The Regis Collection, Minneapolis, Minnesota

Farnham 1959, painting no. 377; Eiseman, no. 3.1920

Provenance: Daniel Gallery, New York; Dr. and Mrs. William Carlos Williams, Rutherford, New Jersey; Mr. and Mrs. Paul H. Williams, Mantoloking, New Jersey; The Regis Collection, 1982

The poet William Carlos Williams, who once owned this painting, was a close friend of Demuth. Williams visited Demuth when he was confined to the sanitorium in Morristown, New Jersey, as well as in Lancaster, and Demuth was a guest at the poet's home in Rutherford, New Jersey. Williams acquired other works by Demuth: *The Gossips*, c. 1914 (Museum of Art of Ogunquit, Ogunquit, Maine; Farnham 1959, painting no. 84), *Pink Lady Slippers*, 1918 (private collection; Farnham 1959, painting no. 333), and *Tuberoses*, 1922 (private collection; Farnham 1959, painting no. 432). The two men's contact was an important factor in their respective artistic productions: Williams dedicated his book of poems *Spring and All* (1923) to Demuth, and one of the painter's best known works is a poster portrait of Williams entitled *I Saw the Figure Five in Gold*, 1928 (The Metropolitan Museum of Art, New York; Farnham 1959, painting no. 515). It was inspired by a poem by Williams, "The Great Figure," first published in *Sour Grapes* in 1920. Demuth dedicated another painting, *Machinery (For W. Carlos W.)*, 1920 (The Metropolitan Museum of Art; Farnham 1959, painting no. 385) to the poet. At the painter's death, Williams wrote an elegy, "The Crimson Cyclamen," to his friend (*see* no. 37). For more discussion of their interaction, *see* Bram Dijkstra, *The Hieroglyphics of a New Speech: Cubism, Stieglitz, and the Early Poetry of William Carlos Williams* (Princeton, 1969); James E. Breslin, "William Carlos Williams and Charles Demuth: Cross-Fertilization in the Arts," *Journal of Modern Language*, vol. 6, no. 2 (April 1977), pp. 248–63; and Tashjian 1978.

End of the Parade may have inspired a poem of the same title by Williams:

The sentence undulates
raising no song—
It is too old, the
words of it are falling
apart. Only percussion
strokes continue
with weakening
emphasis what was once
cadenced melody
full of sweet breath

(William Carlos Williams, "The End of the Parade," from *The Wedge*, 1944, published in *The Collected Later Poems of William Carlos Williams* [New York, 1950], p. 45; *see* James Guimond, *The Art of William Carlos Williams: A Discovery and Possession of America* [Urbana, Ill., 1968], p. 7n).

The subject of this picture is the Lukens Steel Company (fig. 9), located in Coatesville, Pennsylvania, one of the stops for trains running between Lancaster and Philadelphia. Demuth's frequent trips to Philadelphia and New York would have made him familiar with the mill. Lukens Steel is one of the oldest mills in Pennsylvania, having operated on its present site since 1810, though its antecedents date back to the late eighteenth century. Rather than recording any structures that can be specifically identified, Demuth sought to convey a composite of typical forms from the mill complex, which also inspired *Incense of a New Church* (no. 21). The artist occasionally used this approach when painting Lancaster subjects (*see In the Province* [no. 16] and *"After All"* [no. 35]).

Some critics were confused by the title, not knowing quite how to interpret it: "They were very skeptical too about the picture entitled Parade. Mr. Gallatin calls this picture Smoke Stacks. But I think it's called Parade. It may be called Marching Through Georgia. You can't tell about Mr. Demuth's pictures. It all depends on how his whimsy happens to be playing at the moment" (Watson 1923, p. 77).

Others were fascinated by Demuth's depiction of "those precise flowers known as smokestacks" (Louis Kalonyme, "The Art Makers: Charles Demuth, the Magician of Water Colors Leads Art Season of Old Favorites and New Contenders," *Arts and Decoration*, vol. 26, no. 2 [December 1926], p. 63). Most perceptive was the art critic Henry McBride, who declared this painting "one of the most important pictures in modern American art. . . . When a modern mill, with its lofty smoke-stacks and concrete-and-iron walls, falls within his vision, there is no doubt whatever that one side of Mr. Demuth's nature is up in arms—but *que voulez-vous?*—the other side of him is pure artist, and the result, in spite of the concrete, is beautiful" (McBride 1921, p. 235). When *End of the Parade* was exhibited at the Daniel Gallery in New York, McBride wrote admiringly, observing that Demuth "arranges his impressions of the unspeakable buildings in which our American dollars are gained into a lovely report." He felt that Demuth's painting gave Coatesville "an excuse for having existed" and recommended it "to mill owners and muralists for purposes of study" (Henry McBride, *New York Herald*, December 5, 1920).

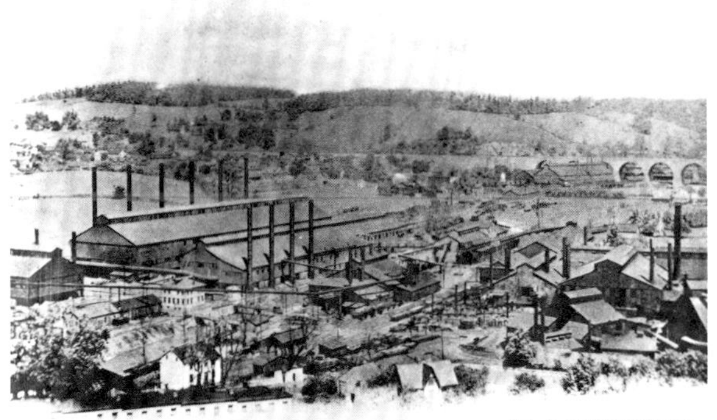

Fig. 9. View of Lukens Steel Company buildings, c. 1920 (Lukens, Inc.)

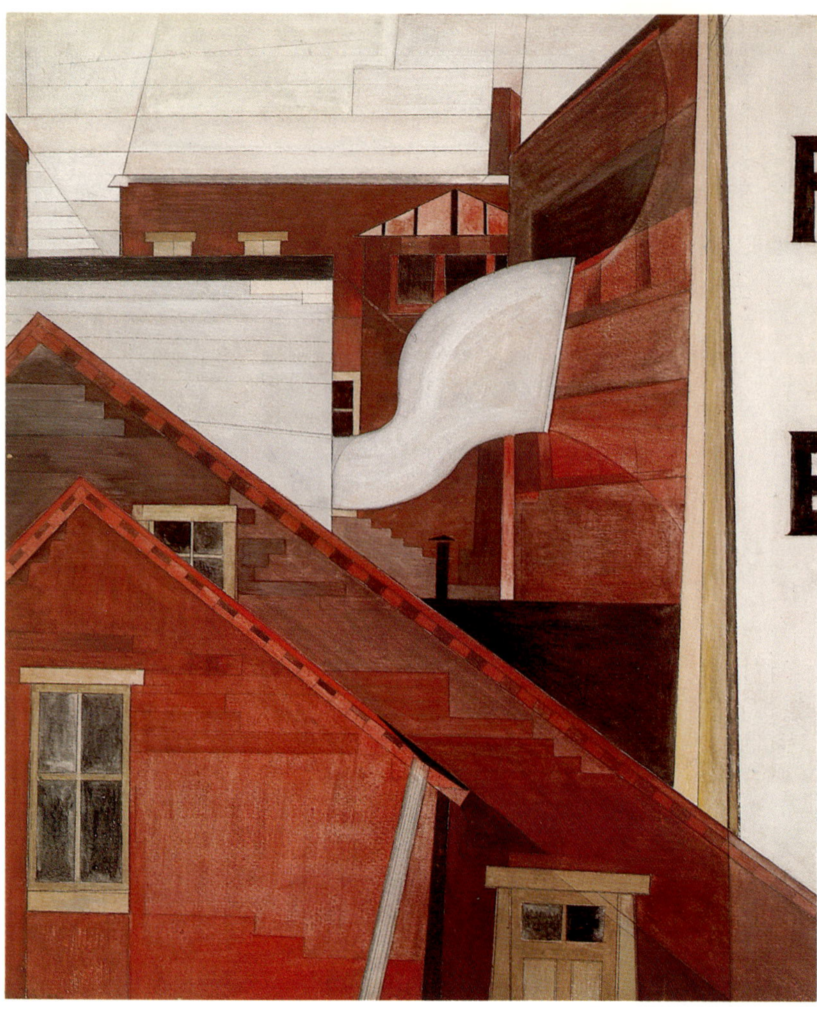

16. In the Province (Roofs), 1920

Tempera and pencil on composition board, 23⅛ x 19³⁄₁₆″ (58.7 x 48.7 cm)

Signed and inscribed, lower left: Demuth—1920, Lancaster, Pa.

Museum of Fine Arts, Boston. Anonymous gift in memory of Nathaniel Saltonstall. 68:790

Farnham 1959, painting no. 381; Eiseman, no. 4.1920

Provenance: Georgia O'Keeffe, Abiquiu, New Mexico, and New York, 1935; Downtown Gallery, New York; John McAndrew, Wellesley, Massachusetts, 1955 or 1956; Museum of Fine Arts, Boston, 1968

This is one of three works entitled *In the Province* (nos. 13, 14, 16). Despite being designated "#1" by Emily Farnham, it was painted a year after the first (no. 13). In that work, a church spire serves as the central focus, while here the artist was inspired by a typical view from a Lancaster backyard. Two large windowed gables are superimposed on one another close to the picture plane, and a series of flat-roofed structures are arranged in the background. Although still clearly recognizable as buildings, the original images have been simplified and abstracted by the artist in his fascination with the formal array of planes, angles, and lines that the scene presented to him. The structures Demuth depicts here have not been identified, and the artist may have intended to make a composite of several different views rather than to show a specific group of buildings. When Henry McBride observed that Demuth's "themes have been found in Pennsylvania and in New England, and not even Hawthorne has been so painstaking with gables" and that "he draws the sharp clean line of our souvenirs of Sir Christopher Wren with an intensity that suggests an inward rage," he captured the controlled crispness that characterizes

Demuth's views of these early buildings (McBride 1921, p. 235).

Demuth began experimenting with tempera in the late teens. His friend Marsden Hartley observed the changes the new technique allowed in his style: "Demuth has since that time stepped out of the confinement of watercolor pure, over into the field of tempera, which brings it nearer to the sturdier mediums employed in the making of pictures evolving a greater severity of form and a commendable rigidity of line. He has learned like so many moderns that the ruled line offers greater advantages in pictorial structure" (Hartley 1921, p. 100).

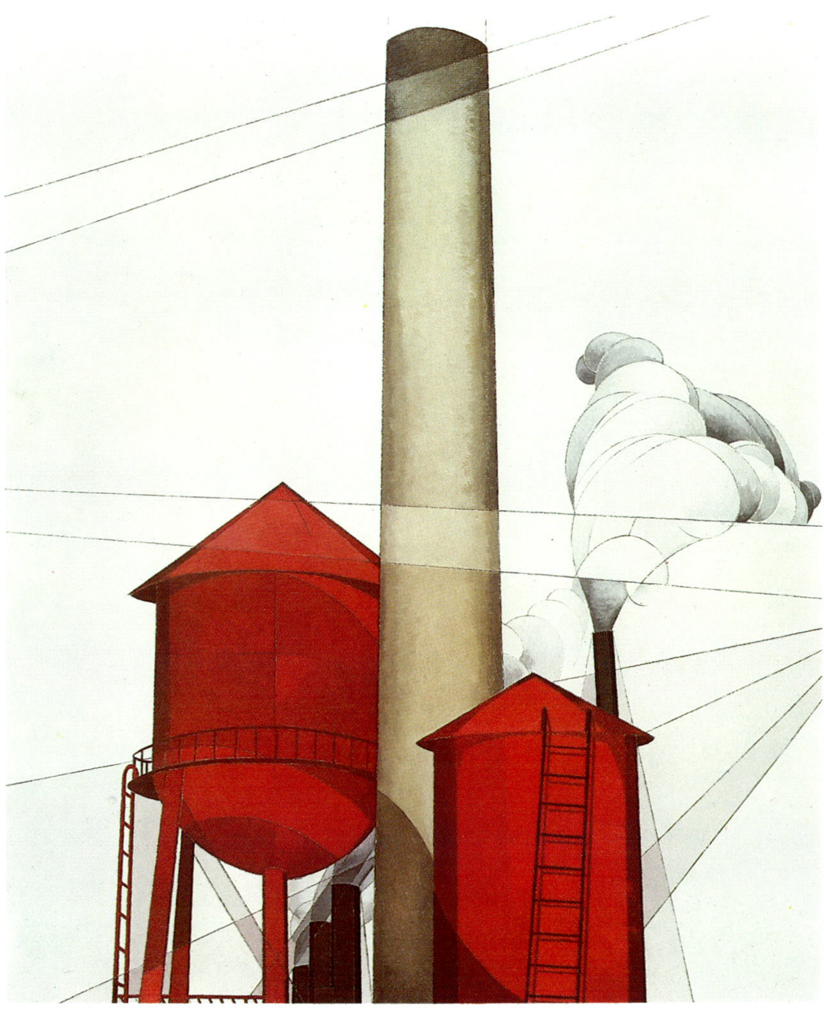

17. Buildings, c. 1920
Tempera and pencil on
composition board,
30 x 24″ (76.2 x 61 cm)

Collection of Audrey
S. Ratner

Farnham 1959,
painting no. 374;
Eiseman, no. 2.1920

Provenance: Muriel Draper,
New York; Raimund
Sanders Draper, New York;
Marcia Ann Draper, New
York; Pamela Draper, New
York; James Maroney,
1977; Audrey S. Ratner,
1978

Muriel Sanders Draper (1886–1952), who was given this picture by the artist, was a friend of both Charles Demuth and Robert Locher. Born in Haverhill, Massachusetts, she was married to the singer Paul Draper, and together they spent considerable time in Paris, where they knew many prominent intellectuals of the period. Her friendship with Gertrude Stein influenced her to adopt Stein's writing style, as is revealed by the following note: "Being here is not being here to not be there where you are you are I am being love and more so" (telegram, Draper to Stein, November 1924[?], Collection of American Literature, The Beinecke Rare Book and Manuscript Library, Yale University, New Haven, Conn.). In return, Stein composed a rather circular word portrait entitled "And So. To Change So. (A Fantasy on Three Careers): Muriel Draper, Yvonne Davidson, Beatrice Locher," in *Portraits and Prayers* (New York, 1934). Mabel Dodge Luhan recorded her recollections of Mrs. Draper in "Muriel," *Intimate Memories* (New York, c. 1933–37), vol. 2, *European Experiences* (1935), pp. 253–73. Muriel Draper herself published some of her memoirs in *Music at Midnight* (New York, 1929); her papers have been deposited at Yale University. In 1927 she

served on a committee to organize an exhibition sponsored by the magazine *The Little Review.* "Machine Age Exposition" opened in May and included at least one work by Demuth, although it is unidentified.

It was not at all unusual for Demuth to present his friends with art works as gifts, but this seems to be the only one based on Lancaster architecture that he gave away, possibly because he made relatively fewer of the building abstractions, which took longer to finish. Unlike some of his architectural works, the specific Lancaster structures shown here have not been identified, although the chimneys and water towers depicted were a common sight in the city. The flattened forms, brilliant red color, and crisp lines dividing and energizing the scene like electrical wires are typical of the artist's industrial views.

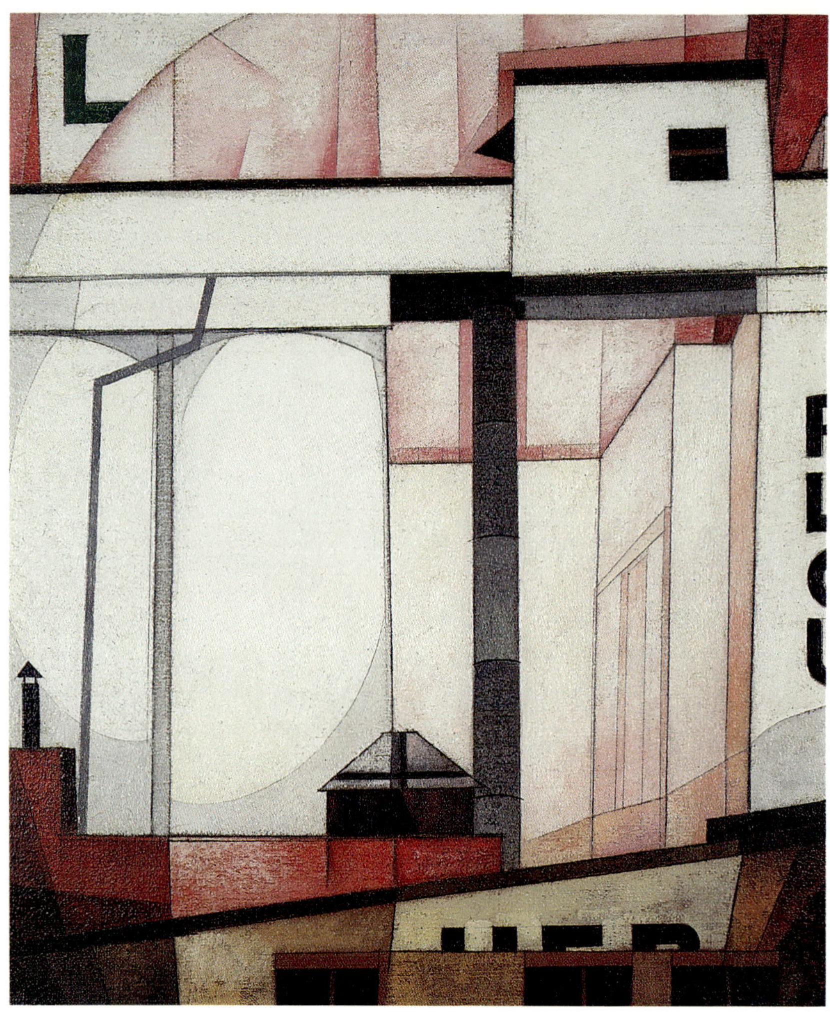

18. Nospmas M. Egiap Nospmas M., 1921

Oil on canvas, 24 x 20"
(61 x 50.8 cm)

Signed and inscribed, verso: 'Nospmas.M.Egiap Nospmas M.'/C. Demuth/ Lancaster, Pa./1921

Munson-Williams-Proctor Institute, Utica, New York. 68.29

Farnham 1959, painting no. 409; Eiseman, no. 9.1921

Provenance: Georgia O'Keeffe[?], Abiquiu, New Mexico, and New York, 1935; Edith Gregor Halpert, New York; Edith Gregor Halpert Foundation; The Downtown Gallery, New York; Munson-Williams-Proctor Institute, 1968

The title has long posed a frustrating riddle to scholars, and while it has been noted that, read backward, the letters form the name "M. Sampson Paige M. Sampson," this intriguing bit of information does not serve to bring us substantially closer to understanding its meaning. It is possible that the name is that of a Lancaster friend, or a person whom Demuth knew or admired in New York, but thus far research has not revealed such an individual. The title may be a bit of deliberate Dada irrationality or may have been applied in the vein of his friend Gertrude Stein's circuitously repetitive prose. One theory is expressed in a letter that quotes an unnamed Lancaster contemporary of Demuth, an expert on his paintings, as saying the title means "page Sampson . . . tear these buildings down" (Mary E. Marshall to the Downtown Gallery, August 22, 1950, Munson-Williams-Proctor Institute, Utica, New York). Eiseman also sees a connection with the Biblical Samson (Eiseman 1976, p. 362).

The careful geometric arrangement of the tall cylindrical forms recalls that of the grain elevators of the John W. Eshelman & Sons feed mills. These structures, since demolished, were on North Queen Street a few blocks from the center of town, and provided the subject for the artist's most famous work, *My Egypt* (no. 29).

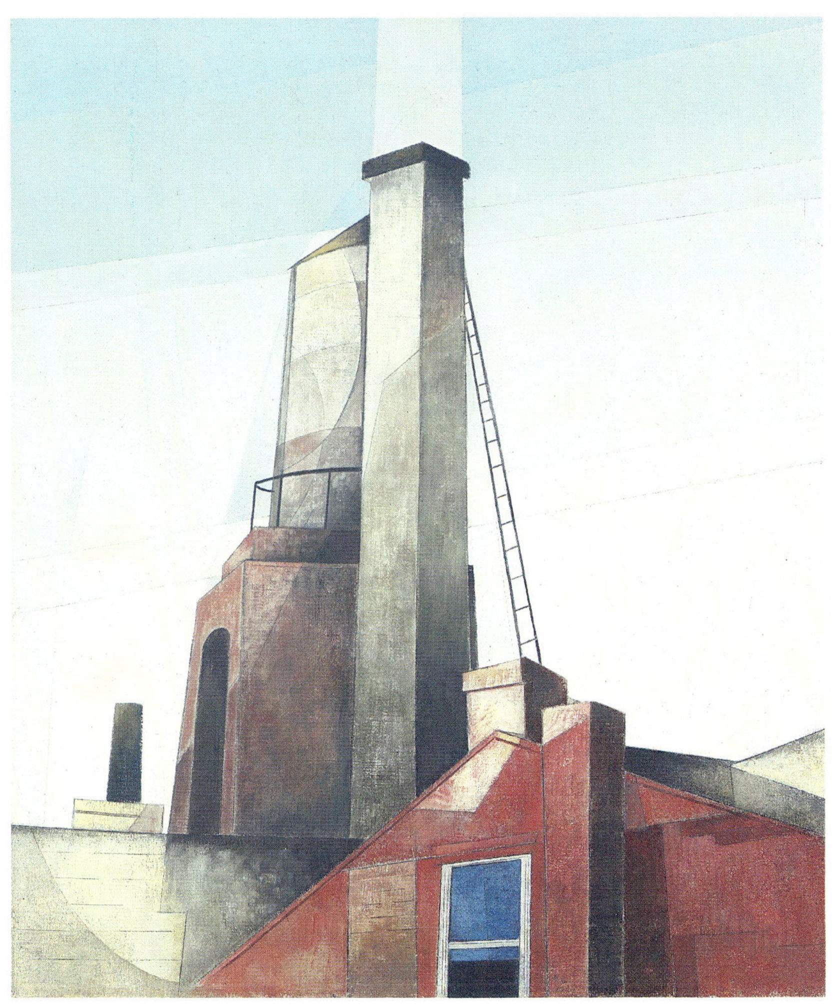

19. Aucassin and Nicolette, 1921
Oil on canvas, 24⅛ x 20"
(61.3 x 50.8 cm)

Signed, verso:
C. Demuth/1921

Columbus Museum of Art,
Columbus, Ohio. Gift of
Ferdinand Howald. 31.123

Farnham 1959, painting no.
398; Eiseman, no. 4.1921

Provenance: Mrs. Meredith
Hare[?], c. 1921; Daniel
Gallery, New York;
Ferdinand Howald, New
York and Columbus, Ohio,
1922; Columbus Gallery of
Fine Arts (now Columbus
Museum of Art), 1931

Forbes Watson commented on the confusion over the title of this painting: "Here's a water tower and a chimney, or whatever they may be, living in silent harmony on a roof, and Mr. Demuth calls them Aucassin and Nicolette. Nearly everyone noted this feat of titular glory when he had his exhibition last month. We had the greatest difficulty convincing our indispensable proof-readers that this title actually belongs to the picture under which it is printed. Can anyone blame them?" (Watson 1923, p. 77). Some critics were not amused, however: "The *jeu d'esprit* is no doubt harmless, but it is not particularly interesting" (Royal Cortissoz, in Samuel Isham, *The History of American Painting* [New York, 1927], p. 591). Later, Cortissoz still maintained his low opinion of the work: "He depicts a tall chimney pressed close against a tower and calls the result *Aucassin and Nicolette*. It is momentarily amusing, but the jape is really rather feeble, and it is quite powerless to lift the subject into the sphere of pictorial interest" (Royal Cortissoz, "The Delicate Art of the Late Charles Demuth," *New York Herald Tribune*, December 19, 1937). The critic Albert E. Gallatin, was, however, pleased with the controversy this work incited: "One recalls,

with great satisfaction, the uproar and indignation this title caused in academic circles" (Gallatin 1927, p. 8).

Like many of Demuth's architectural works based on Lancaster themes, *Aucassin and Nicolette* was not readily appreciated by most critics, because of a preference for his vaudeville and still-life themes as well as a failure to grasp the full iconographic and artistic richness of this painting.

The theme is based on a medieval French story of two persecuted lovers, which is recounted succinctly by Karal Ann Marling: "The romance sung by the thirteenth-century minstrel tells the story of Aucassin, barred by his aristocratic father from marriage to Nicolette, a beautiful girl of unknown parentage, ransomed from the Saracens. The wicked Count de Beaucaire imprisons her in a tower; when she manages to escape, Nicolette is pursued by soldiers of the watch and takes refuge in the shadows of another ruined tower, in which Aucassin languishes. Their whispered reunion presages eventual marriage, after countless trials and travels" (Marling 1980, p. 32n).

Demuth transforms the imagery of the tale into twentieth-century terms, depicting Aucassin and Nicolette as a smokestack and a water tower. The water tower has been identified as part of an old Lancaster textile mill, later the P. Lorillard Company tobacco factory, depicted the previous year by Demuth in *In the Province* (no. 14). S. Lane Faison, Jr., has also located the smokestack in the Lorillard complex (*see* Faison 1950, pp. 124–25). As in that work, Demuth has altered the view, placing next to each other structures that did not exist in such close proximity in the actual cityscape. The artist simplified shapes and eliminated non-essential elements to focus attention on the towers. For Demuth, the painting may have symbolized reunion: of Aucassin and Nicolette, but also of Demuth and the poet William Carlos Williams, whom Demuth had known since his student days but whom he saw more often after ill health reduced his social life in New York (Marling 1980, pp. 31–32). Williams later recalled his discovery, while a student, of "the wonders of *Aucassin and Nicolette*, the prose and the verse alternating" (Williams 1951, p. 52), an enthusiasm he must have shared with Demuth. According to Marling, who has made the most thorough analysis of the work to date, it also represents the painter's realization of the precarious nature of his own health, for his diabetes had been recently diagnosed (Marling 1980, pp. 31–32).

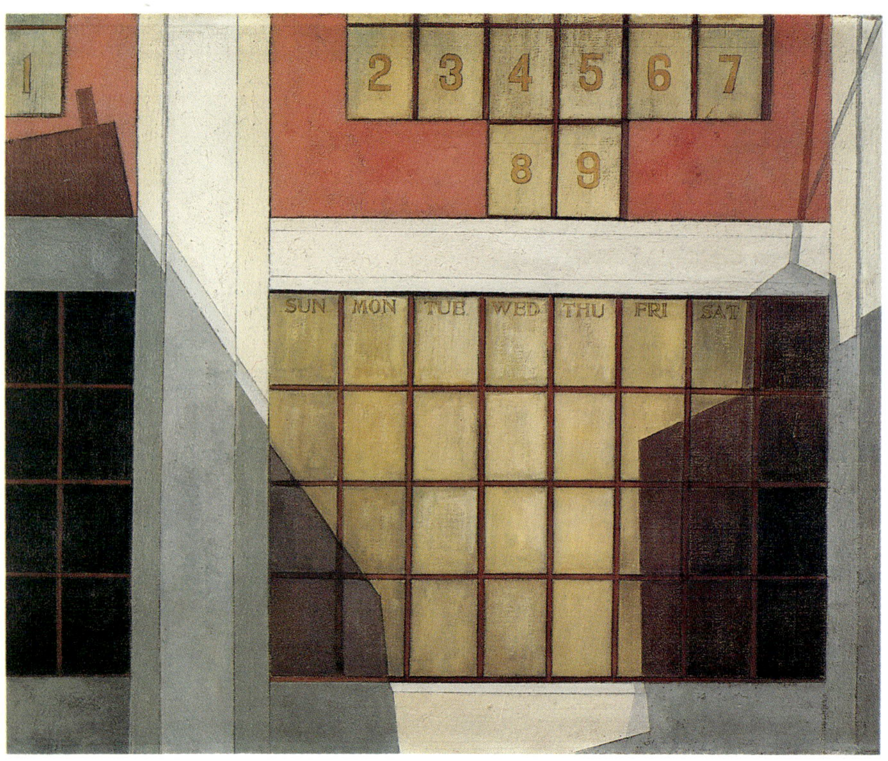

20. Business, 1921
Oil on canvas, 20 x 24"
(50.8 x 61 cm)

Signed and inscribed,
lower left: Demuth, 1921;
verso: C. Demuth./1921
"BUSINESS"

The Alfred Stieglitz
Collection. Lent to the Art
Institute of Chicago by
Georgia O'Keeffe

Farnham 1959, painting
no. 400; Eiseman, no.
5.1921

Provenance: Georgia
O'Keeffe, Abiquiu, New
Mexico, and New York,
1935; The Art Institute of
Chicago, on extended
loan, 1949

In this painting, an unusually strong geometric composition for Demuth, the grid pattern created by the window wall of a commercial structure dominates the surface, creating a strong design element. In the insistent flatness of the surface, *Business* is similar to *Spring*, c. 1916 (The Solomon R. Guggenheim Museum; Farnham 1959, painting no. 209), Demuth's only totally abstract painting, and heralds the graphic two-dimensionality of the poster portraits of the 1920s. Some of the panes contain the numbers one through ten, others abbreviations for the days of the week, each in a separate rectangle. Shadows of other industrial structures are reflected in the windows. Although the shadowed forms depicted in this painting correspond to several buildings in Lancaster, Emily Farnham noted a resemblance to the Lancaster Laundry, a building visible from the artist's studio window (Farnham 1959, p. 568). *Business* was one of several oil paintings left to Georgia O'Keeffe at Demuth's death in 1935.

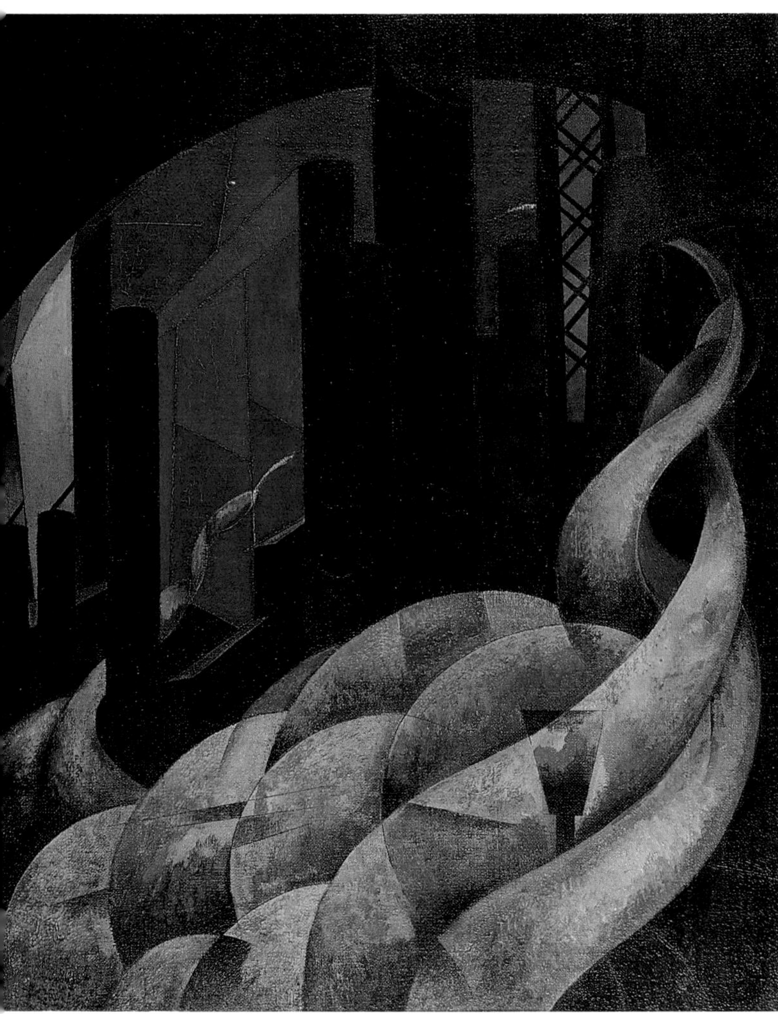

Taking its inspiration from the same source as *End of the Parade: Coatesville, Pa.* (no. 15), *Incense of a New Church* too draws its visual motifs from the Lukens Steel factory in nearby Coatesville, a site Demuth glimpsed frequently on his train journeys to Philadelphia and New York. Prominently visible from the train, the vertical smokestacks as depicted by Demuth are more numerous and closer together than they actually were, compared with other structures from the factory complex. Like the earlier painting, *Incense of a New Church* does not record any specifically identifiable structures, reflecting instead an imaginative interpretation of the site. With the exception of *My Egypt* (no. 29), the structures Demuth painted in Lancaster and its environs were all quite old, in harmony with the community and bearing strong historical associations for him. (Although Lukens Steel had undergone considerable expansion during Demuth's lifetime, the business was founded in the nineteenth century.)

Thus, the comparative darkness of this work might appear to indicate condemnation of the effect on the rural landscape of this, the heaviest industry in the area, but the style Demuth adopted does not support such an interpretation. He transforms the steel yards into a grand organ-like panoply of smokestacks, the smoke swirling like incense throughout, evoking a grand cathedral-like space. The forms are treated not as threats to the ecology but as fascinating visual elements, abstracted and transmogrified from the original reference into something undeniably sublime in modern terms. As in *My Egypt*, Demuth raises an ordinary scene to one of mythic dimension.

21. Incense of a New Church, 1921
Oil on canvas, 26 x 20⅛"
(66 x 51.1 cm)

Signed and inscribed, verso: "Incense of a new/ Church."/C. Demuth./ Lancaster, Pa./1921

Columbus Museum of Art, Columbus, Ohio. Gift of Ferdinand Howald. 31.135

Farnham 1959, painting no. 406; Eiseman, no. 7.1921

Provenance: Daniel Gallery, New York; Ferdinand Howald, New York and Columbus, Ohio, 1923; Columbus Gallery of Fine Arts (now Columbus Museum of Art), 1931

Incense of a New Church was originally purchased by Ferdinand Howald (1856–1934), an avant-garde collector from Columbus whose considerable collection of American art launched that museum in 1931 (*see* Columbus, Ohio, Columbus Gallery of Fine Arts, *American Paintings in the Ferdinand Howald Collection* [Columbus, 1969]). Beginning his collection in 1916, with a purchase of six watercolors for seventy-five dollars from the Daniel Gallery in New York, one of the most advanced dealers then operating in New York, Howald eventually owned twenty-eight works by Demuth (*see* Mahonri Sharp Young, "Ferdinand Howald: The Art of the Collector," *Apollo*, n.s. vol. 90, no. 92 [October 1969], p. 341). Through his purchases of works by Demuth and others, Howald established himself as Daniel's most important client (*see* Elizabeth McCausland, "The Daniel Gallery and Modern American Art," *Magazine of Art*, vol. 44, no. 7 [November 1951], pp. 280–85).

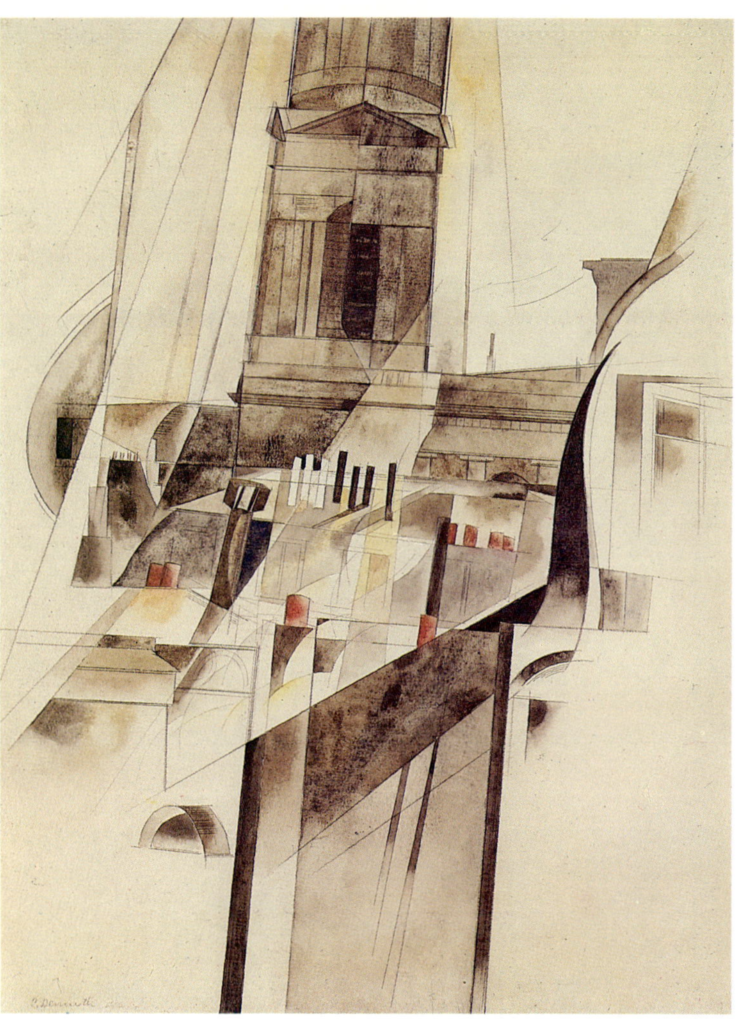

22. Roofs and Steeple,
1921

Watercolor and pencil on
paper, 14¼ x 10⅜"
(36.2 x 26.4 cm)

Signed, lower left:
C. Demuth 1921

The Brooklyn Museum,
Brooklyn, New York. Dick
S. Ramsay Fund. 50.159

Farnham 1959, painting no.
412; Eiseman, no. 21.1921

Provenance: Robert Locher,
Lancaster, 1935; Kraushaar
Galleries, New York;
Charles D. Childs Gallery,
Boston, 1942; The Brooklyn
Museum, 1950

In this watercolor, Demuth focused on a great tower centered above fragmented forms. The use of watercolor rather than tempera produces more subdued colors than the bright primary reds and yellows usually found in the artist's works based on Lancaster architecture. The steeple that inspired this work is that of Trinity Lutheran Church, on East Mifflin Street, directly behind the Demuth home in Lancaster. Demuth's father, Ferdinand, an amateur photographer, took a one-hour exposure of the tower by moonlight (fig. 10). Although the congregation was founded in 1738, and remains the oldest in the city, the church painted by Demuth was built considerably later. Demuth's mother was a member of the church and Charles is thought to have painted a star in its steeple, though it has long since disappeared (Farnham 1959, p. 19). At her death in 1943,

Demuth's mother, Augusta, left the church almost $17,000 to be used to install two windows in memory of her parents and her two sisters and to keep the steeple painted.

In discussing several similar paintings of this steeple, Henry McBride commented on the appeal Demuth's works held for viewers espousing a wide variety of artistic tastes: "For instance, many persons who condemn cubism as the sin of all sins, have openly admired the several water color versions of Sir Christopher Wren church steeples without seeming to be aware that the drawings are cubistic. It is quite refined and delicate cubism but it is cubism just the same" (Henry McBride, "Demuth Memorial Exhibition," *New York Sun*, December 18, 1937).

Demuth's interest in painting Wren-style churches has caused some confusion in identification. One depiction of Trinity Lutheran Church, *After Sir Christopher Wren (New England)*, 1920 (Worcester Art Museum; Farnham 1959, painting no. 372), had long been considered to represent the Universalist Church in Provincetown. This author discovered the incorrect identification by comparing the painting with the two churches. Furthermore, *The Tower (After Sir Christopher Wren)*, 1920 (Columbus Museum of Art; Farnham 1959, painting no. 395; Eiseman, no. 7.1920) depicts the Provincetown church rather than Trinity Lutheran Church in Lancaster

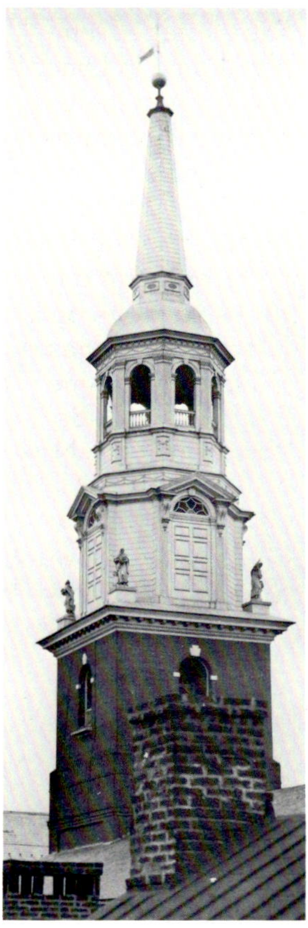

Fig. 10. Trinity Lutheran Church steeple, by Ferdinand Demuth, c. 1900 (Private Collection)

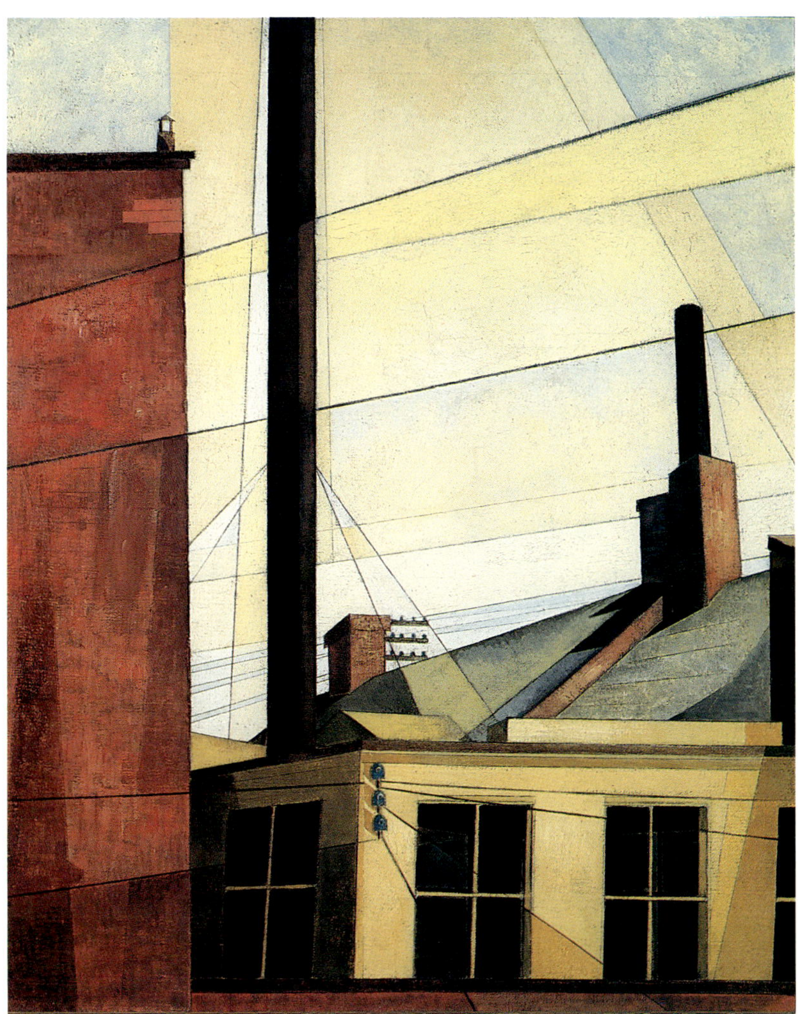

The château Demuth refers to in the title is his own home in Lancaster, a modest structure dating from the eighteenth century. Demuth's garden was important as a place in which to relax and a source of subject matter for his art. Yet its central role in his life did not prevent him from regarding it with a certain wry humor, as he revealed in a letter: "I am back in the province in the garden of my own château" (Demuth to Agnes and Eugene O'Neill, 1919, Collection of American Literature, The Beinecke Rare Book and Manuscript Library, Yale University, New Haven, Conn.) The garden referred to in the title is not visible in this work, however, since its vantage point is an upper window in his house. Rather, he focuses on nearby structures, chimneys, and electrical wires, which he transforms into a subtly colored flat pattern of planes and abstract forms.

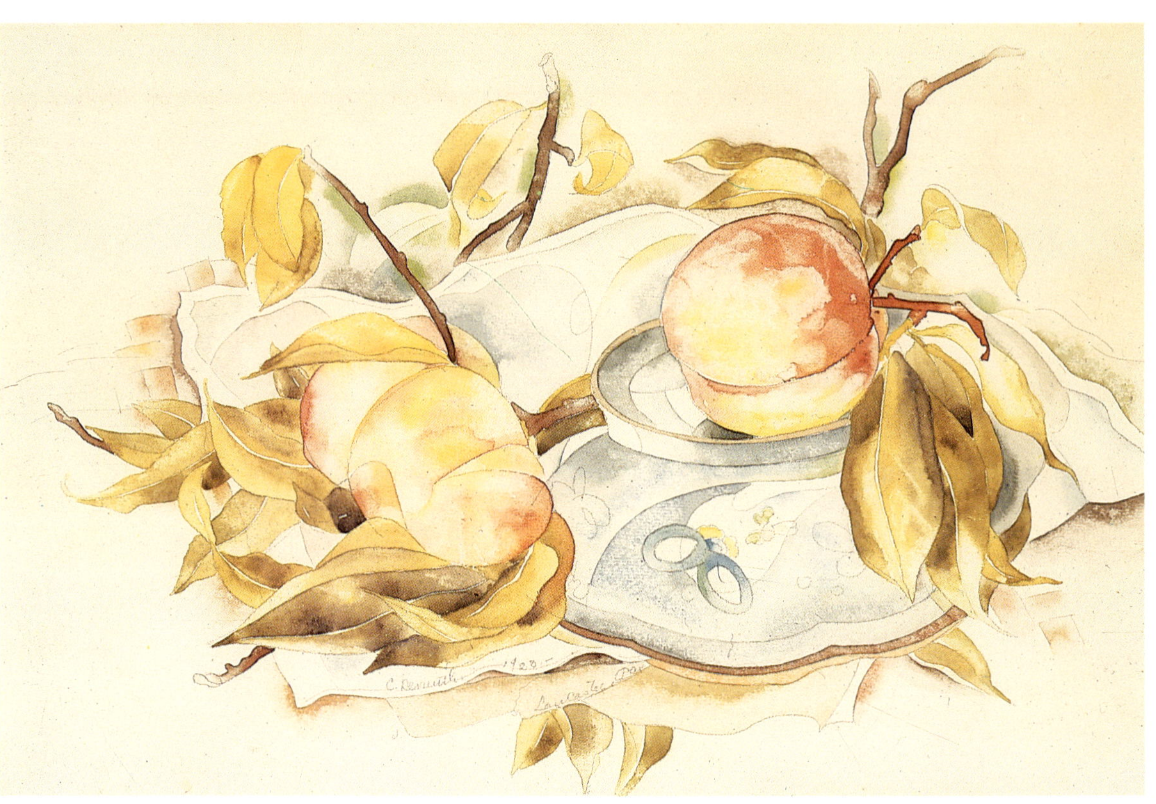

Of the great early modern collectors who acquired Demuth's work, such as Albert Barnes, Ferdinand Howald, and Louise and Walter Arensberg, one of the most important was Albert E. Gallatin (1881–1952). His collection eventually included major works by Arp, Braque, Cézanne, Léger, Mondrian, and Picasso, as well as American modernists such as Demuth, Marin, Sheeler, Ilya Bolotowsky, Suzy Frelinghuysen, Fritz Glarner, and George L. K. Morris. His Gallery of Living Art, which opened at New York University in 1927, was the first museum devoted to contemporary art in America. Although Charles Daniel claimed that Gallatin was "petty and a bargain hunter" and that he and Demuth "never got along together" (quoted in Farnham 1959, p. 994), he was nonetheless a longtime admirer of Demuth and came to own several important works. Gallatin wrote enthusiastically on Demuth in his *American Water-Colourists* (New York, 1922) and five years later published *Charles Demuth* (New York, 1927), the first monograph on the artist.

Demuth left few comments on specific works, feeling that his paintings were self-explanatory: "Across the final surface—the touchable bloom, if it were a peach—of any fine painting is written for those who dare to read that which the painter knew, that which he hoped to find out, or, that which he—whatever! (Demuth 1929, pp. 629, 634). In this work Demuth revealed his consummate skill in watercolor, delicately placing layers of pink to create the roundness of the fruit, adding a tinge of yellow, arranging the peaches against clusters of carefully curved green leaves, and always preserving a remarkable transparency of color.

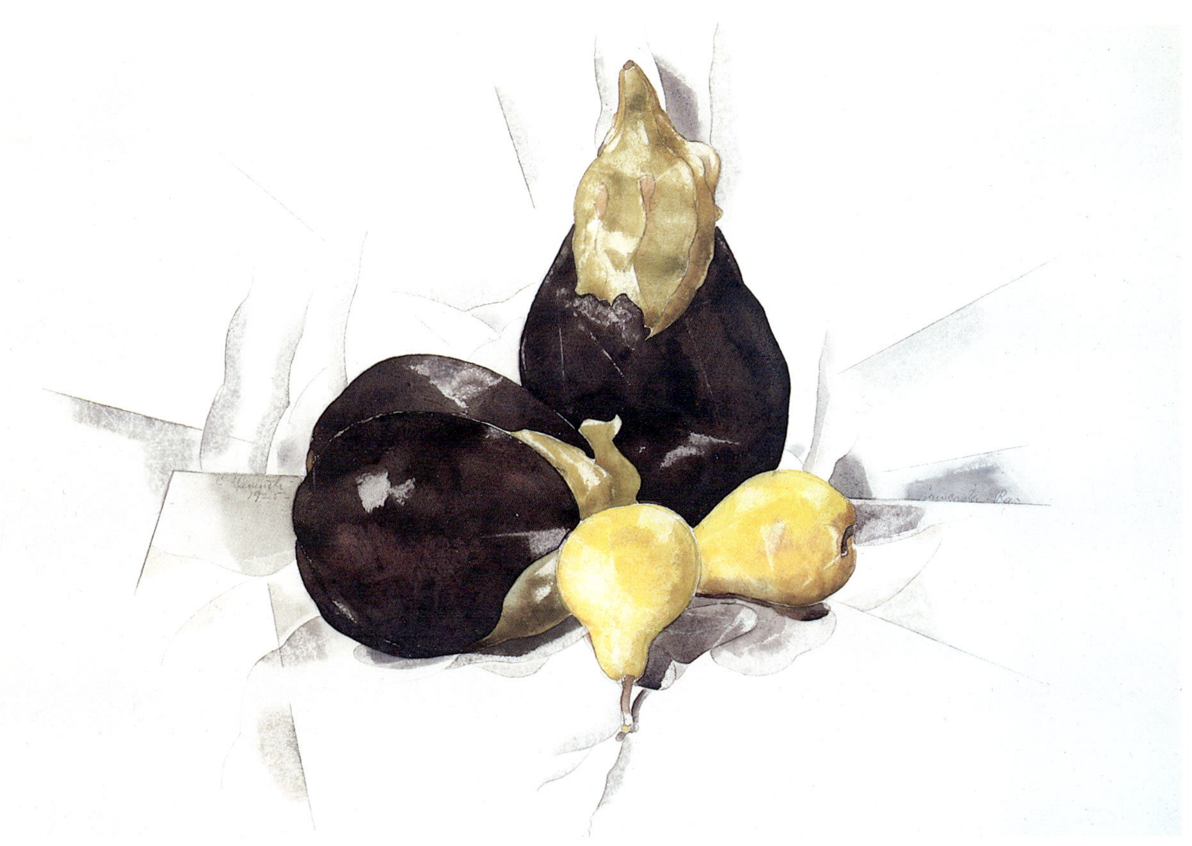

25. Eggplants and Pears, 1925
Watercolor and pencil on paper, 13⅝ x 19⁹⁄₁₆"
(34.6 x 49.7 cm)

Signed at left, in image: C. Demuth—/ 1925—; inscribed at right, in image: Lancaster, Pa.

Museum of Fine Arts, Boston. Bequest of John T. Spaulding. 48.765

Farnham 1959, painting no. 461; Eiseman, no. 9.1925

Provenance: John T. Spaulding, Boston; Museum of Fine Arts, 1948

Charles Demuth's mother, Augusta, shopped regularly at Lancaster farmers' markets, arriving early in the morning for the best selection of fresh produce. The vegetables and fruit she purchased often became subjects for her son's watercolors. The Demuth home at 118 East King Street is within a few blocks of two of Lancaster's most active markets, both housed in late nineteenth-century structures. Central Market, the closest, is one of the oldest farmers' markets in the United States, and Southern Market is nearby.

The artist's comments to Alfred Stieglitz concerning an earlier watercolor of an eggplant are generally applicable to Demuth's approach to still-life painting: "I'm glad you want the eggplant—I kept it here; it turned into a heart;—maybe mine; anyway I hope no one will discover 'Art' or 'Painting' engraved on it" (Demuth to Stieglitz, January 29, 1923, Collection of American Literature, The Beinecke Rare Book and Manuscript Library, Yale University, New Haven, Conn.). Although Demuth painted many still lifes containing eggplants, this is the only one that is signed and dated as well as having Lancaster inscribed on it. Henry McBride admired "the glittering polish of the aubergine" (McBride 1929, p. 635), and this is one of the artist's most striking compositions featuring that vegetable. The forms are arranged in a strongly centralized composition, the geometric line of the cloth providing a perfect foil for the rich purple of the eggplants.

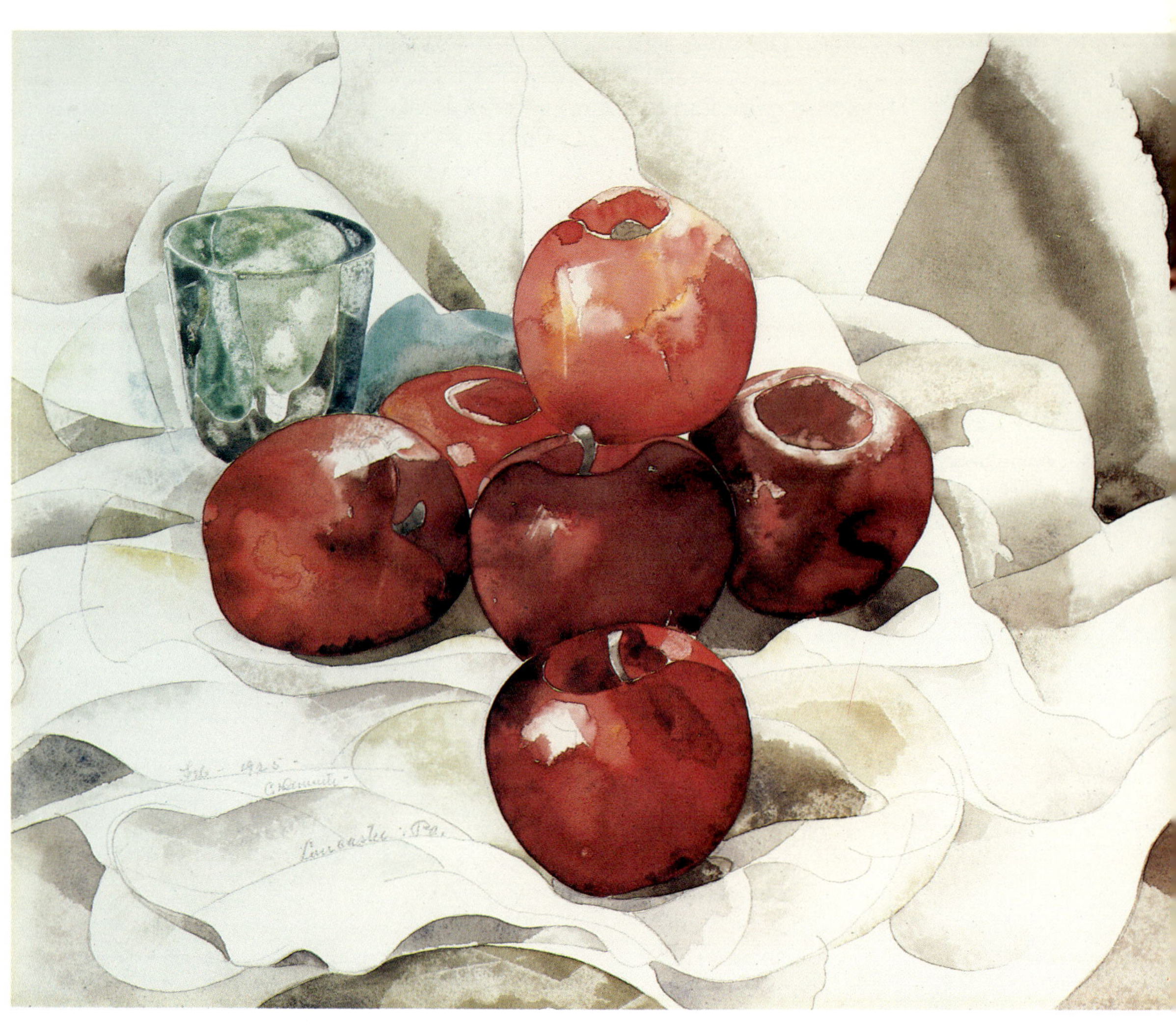

26. Apples and Green Glass, 1925
Watercolor and pencil on paper, 11¹³⁄₁₆ x 13¾"
(30 x 34.9 cm)

Signed and inscribed, lower left: Feb—1925—/ C. Demuth—/Lancaster, Pa.

The Art Institute of Chicago. Olivia Shaler Swan Memorial Collection. 1933.473

Farnham 1959, painting no. 281; Eiseman, no. 23.1925

Provenance: Annie Swan (Mrs. L. L.) Coburn, Chicago; The Art Institute of Chicago, 1933

One of Demuth's most accomplished still lifes, *Apples and Green Glass* presents a brilliantly colored grouping of six apples against a crumpled cloth. The artist's facility with the watercolor medium is evident in his carefully handled reds, which allow bits of the paper to show through, with yellow added for highlights and brown for stems and for defining the edges of shapes. To the left of the apples, Demuth placed a green glass tumbler of the sort that may have inspired an unnamed critic in 1931 to admire "his carefully compounded studies of flowers and fruits, wrought in his particular way of condensed water coloring much like the precious jade and crystal carvings of the Chinese" ("Charles Demuth, An American Place," *Art News*, vol. 29, no. 29 [April 18, 1931], p. 10). As in many of his still lifes, the central forms are more fully realized and less abstract than are those in the background, where he permitted more of the underlying pencil sketch to show through. Some critics preferred his flower still lifes to those composed of fruits and vegetables, as Gallatin revealed: "These still-lifes are very handsome and take their place with the artist's finest things. It is possible, however, that certain of Demuth's admirers find more charm in the flower subjects, with their note of graciousness. These fruits and vegetables are very cool. The juiciness of a peach by Renoir or the passion which Cézanne put into an apple are not to be found here. This is not voluptuous fruit: it comes from a country whose *vin du paye* [sic] is iced water" (Gallatin 1927, p. 9).

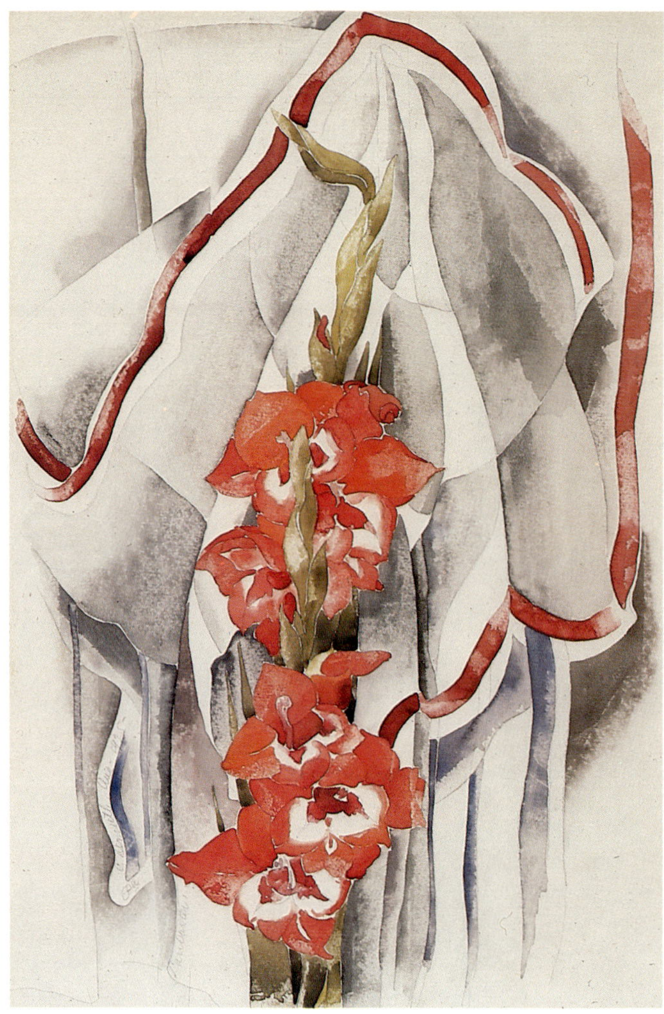

**27. Red Gladioli and
Napkin,** 1925
Watercolor and pencil
on paper, 18 x 12"
(45.7 x 30.5 cm)

Signed and inscribed,
lower left: C. Demuth.
Aug—1925—/
Lancaster, Pa.

The Santa Barbara
Museum of Art, Santa
Barbara, California. Gift of
Wright S. Ludington.
1945.6.6

Farnham 1959, painting no.
477; Eiseman, no. 19.1925

Provenance: Robert Locher,
Lancaster, 1935; Kraushaar
Galleries, New York;
Wright S. Ludington; The
Santa Barbara Museum of
Art, 1945

Of all Demuth's works, flower paintings were
the most highly sought after by private
collectors and museums, though the artist
never took advantage of the situation:
"Charles Demuth, too, spoke seldom. That is,
he used the language of flowers too seldom to
please his admirers. Nevertheless, a few private
collections of art have been made distinguished
by priceless bouquets from his garden, and I
believe most of the public museums have tried
to perfume certain alcoves in the same way.
The bleak air of the museums, however, is
rather cruel to such tenderness and the proper
place for a Demuth flower, I sometimes think, is
in the hands of an educated gardener—one
who knows what a flower is and what an artist
is" (McBride 1938, p. 21).

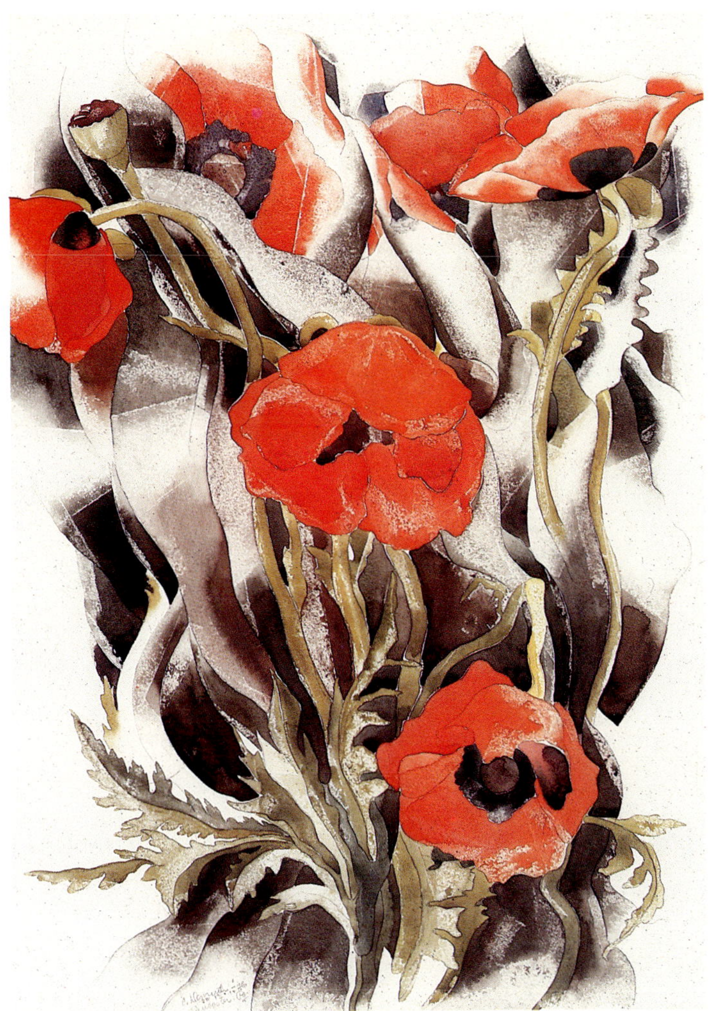

28. Poppies, 1926
Watercolor and pencil on paper, 28½ x 21½"
(72.4 x 54.6 cm)

Signed and inscribed, lower left:
C. Demuth—'26/
Lancaster, Pa.

The Santa Barbara Museum of Art, Santa Barbara, California. Gift of Wright S. Ludington. 1945.6.4

Farnham 1959, painting no. 492; Eiseman, no. 8.1926

Provenance: Kraushaar Galleries, New York; Frank Crowninshield, New York, 1927; Wright S. Ludington; The Santa Barbara Museum of Art, 1945

Flowers provided a continuing source of inspiration for Demuth, from the late teens until the end of his career. Part of their attraction had to do with the pleasure he found in working in his family's garden, which flourished at the back of his house in Lancaster, beneath his studio window: "Watercolor was his favorite medium; it fitted his exquisite tastes, and with it he expressed with extraordinary precision and delicacy of perception the things that interested him most. Flowers endlessly fascinated him. They were in the family, as it were. His mother kept a luxuriant Victorian garden which is still the glory of the Demuth house in Lancaster" (Ritchie 1950, pp. 6–7).

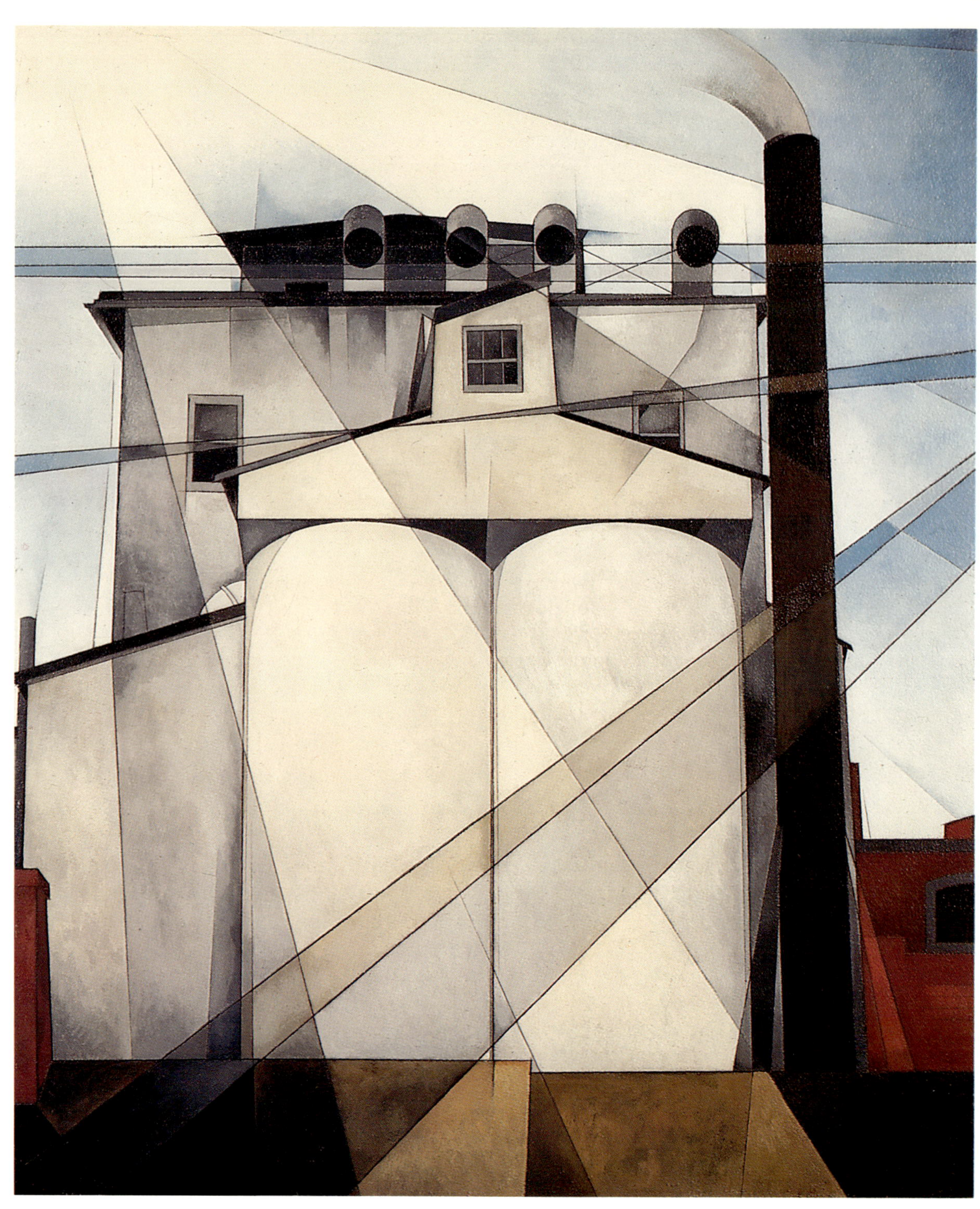

Surely Charles Demuth's most famous work, if not the best understood, *My Egypt* remains one of the most compelling yet elusive images in American art of the first half of the twentieth century. Although a great deal has been written on this painting, its full iconographic richness was not revealed until the publication of an insightful article by Karal Ann Marling, in which she stated that *My Egypt* was "a culminating reprise of themes, methods, and relationships pieced together in a biographical context haunted by the shadow of death" (Marling 1980, p. 32).

Erected in 1919 on the foundation of a structure dating back to 1842, the reinforced concrete grain elevators of the John W. Eshelman & Sons feed mills, the painting's subject, stood at 244 North Queen Street in Lancaster. They represented a modern addition to the skyline of Lancaster, symbolic of the strength of the local agricultural industry. The structures were demolished in 1978 to expand the headquarters of the Lancaster Association for the Blind, owners of the former Eshelman complex, which also inspired *Buildings, Lancaster* (no. 33). This site was a particularly rich one for the artist, for the looming forms atop the grain elevators may have provided the visual motifs for yet another painting, *Waiting (Ventilators)*, 1930 (The Art Institute of Chicago, Farnham 1959, painting

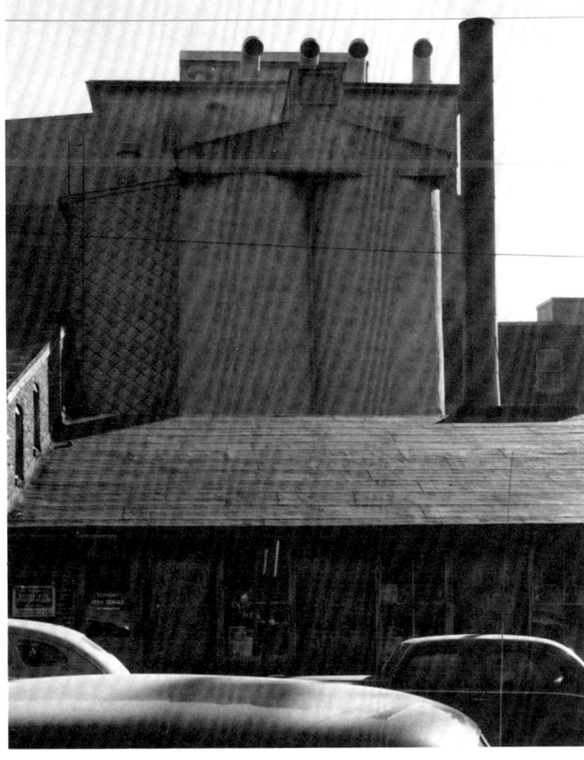

Fig. 11. John W. Eshelman & Sons grain elevators, c. 1950 (Courtesy of S. Lane Faison, Jr.)

no. 550). Demuth's choice of a Lancaster subject for this major work emphasizes the value he placed on heritage. Yet he altered the space of the actual site (see fig. 11), simplifying and adding dynamically intersecting ray-like lines to the strong, functional forms.

One of Demuth's most forceful treatments of an industrial subject, the monumental forms of the grain elevators emphasizes their closeness to monolithic masses like the Pyramids. Perhaps this visual and psychological similarity inspired the title. Marling carries the Pyramid analogy further, noting that by the late twenties Demuth found his health problems increasingly worrisome and his own death approaching nearer. She suggests that *My Egypt*, a late major work, may be read as "Demuth's memorial to himself" (Marling 1980, p. 33) employing the tomb-like simplicity of the grain elevators as a neo-Egyptian symbol of immortality.

The problems of interpretation are not illuminated by a printed statement of uncertain authorship (but not by Alfred Stieglitz) supplied to visitors by the gallery An American Place at a Demuth exhibition held shortly after the artist's death: "in the Whitney museum is a painting by Charles Demuth called 'MY EGYPT'. it represents gift-giving. it is small, obscure, delicate—a study of factory buildings—dextrous, acute, perhaps the finest sense of a modern age that has been expressed. this painting has a history. its history may some day be known. a slow process, this knowing, knowing history. hard to know. the painting may then be seen, be received. hard to see, to receive" ("It Must Be Said," no. 4 (November 1935), An American Place, New York, reproduced in Farnham 1971, p. 161).

When the Whitney Museum of American Art bought *My Egypt*, Demuth was pleased to have the work enter a major museum collection, and wrote to Juliana Force, the first director of the museum, "It is one of my best things, I think" (Demuth to Force, February 17, 1931, Archives of the Whitney Museum of American Art). He was conscious that it was a major work for him, and, aware of his frail health, was glad to be represented in such a collection by that particular piece. Although Demuth had asked higher prices for other works, the Whitney paid fifteen hundred dollars for the painting, not a negligible sum at the beginning of the Depression.

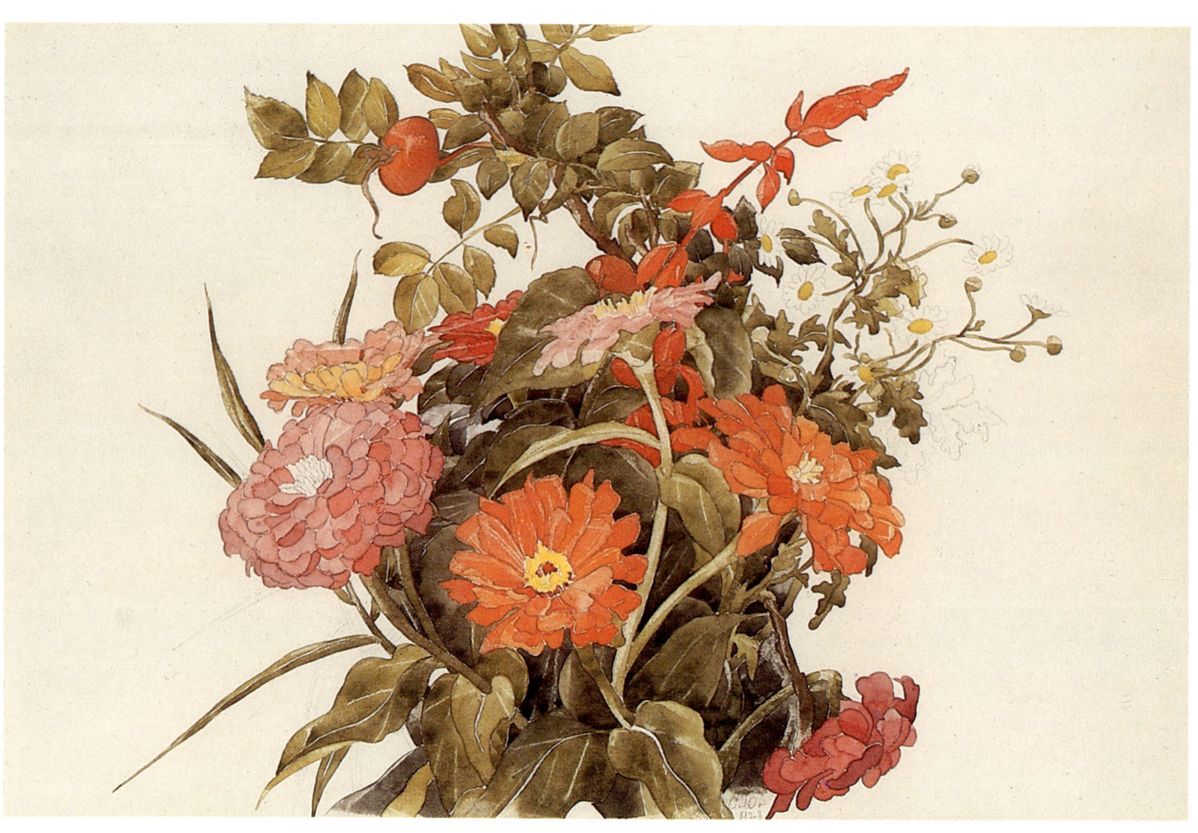

30. Zinnias with Scarlet Sage, 1928
Watercolor and pencil
on paper, 11¹⁵⁄₁₆ x 17¹⁵⁄₁₆"
(30.3 x 45.6 cm)

Signed, lower center:
C.D. 1928

Private Collection, Bird-in-
Hand, Pennsylvania

Farnham 1959, painting
no. 522; Eiseman, no.
13.1928

Provenance: Robert Locher,
Lancaster, 1935; private
collection, 1938

Some of Demuth's still lifes depict a single type of flower; others, like this one, are bouquets of several different plants. Henry McBride admired what he termed "the controlled richness of the opulent zinnias" (McBride 1929, p. 635), certainly evident here in the way the colors have been applied to each petal of the large, handsome blossoms.

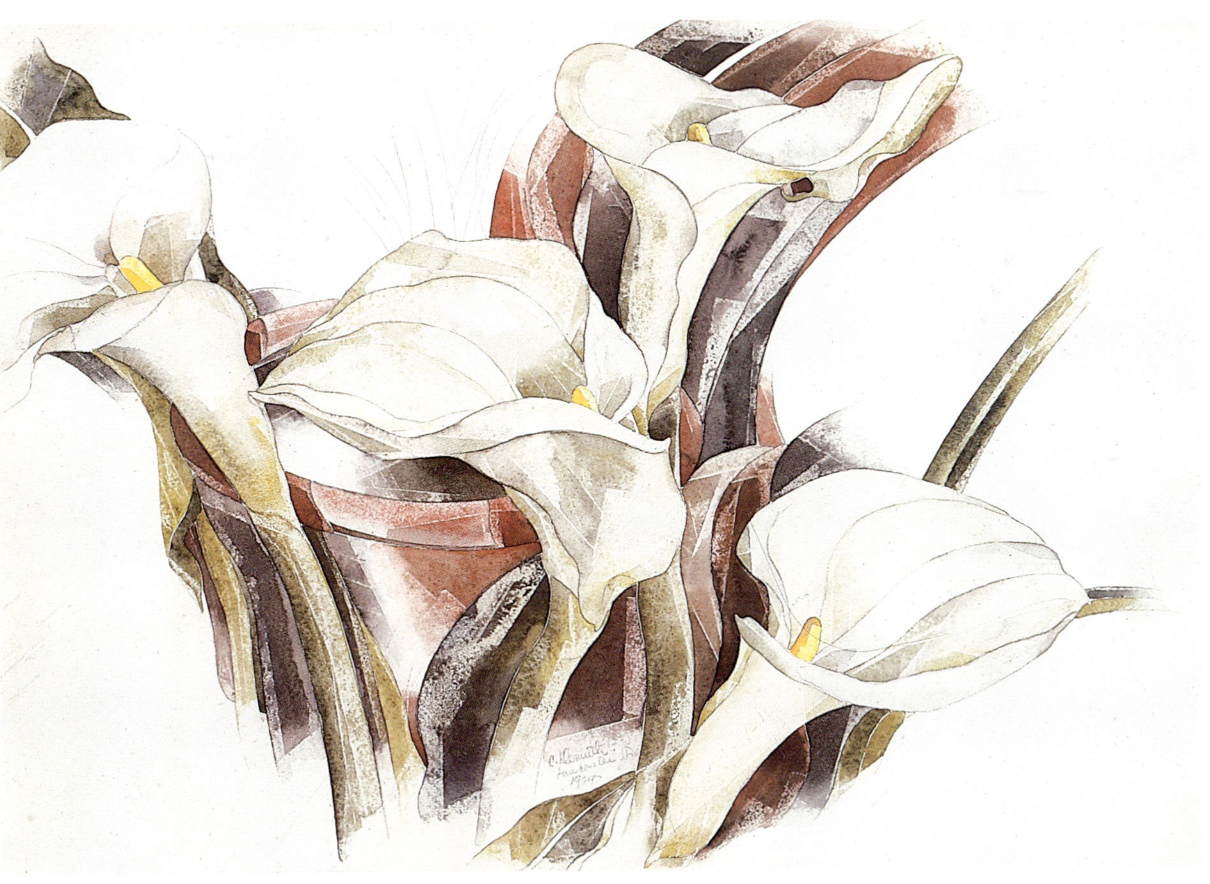

31. Calla Lilies, 1929
Watercolor and pencil on
paper, 13⅞ x 19⅞"
(35.2 x 50.5 cm)

Signed and inscribed,
lower center:
C. Demuth/Lancaster,
Pa./1929

Williams College Museum
of Art, Williamstown,
Massachusetts. Bequest of
Susan W. Street. 57.9

Farnham 1959, painting no.
524; Eiseman, no. 25.1929

Provenance: Robert Locher,
Lancaster, 1935; Susan
Watts Street, New York,
1940; Williams College
Museum of Art, 1957

Some writers expressed the opinion that
Demuth's flowers gave the artist a better
chance to reveal his keen sense of visual order
than his industrial works. Wolfgang Born
noted, "It was the art form of the close-up,
however, in which he expressed himself most
happily. The delicate tangle of weeds, the
silver bells of a set of calla lilies, the pattern of
fruits and foliage in a plum tree—these were
the motifs that gave him the best chance of
developing his innate love of precision, not the
world of steel construction. Very transparent,
subdued, and pure colors add to the dainty
and fastidious effect of his art. Demuth's
precisionism was a subtle guiding force rather
than a principle" (Wolfgang Born, *Still-Life
Painting in America* [New York, 1947], p. 46).

Calla lilies, though more exotic than the
flowers Demuth usually depicted, inspired
several other works, and are prominent in his
1927 poster portrait for Bert Savoy, a popular
female impersonator (Farnham 1959, painting
no. 505). Henry McBride remarked on the
flower that inspired this watercolor, "Just what
it is that makes the Calla so esteemed in these
days, other than the fact that it was considered
vulgar a generation ago, I cannot say, but
possibly that in itself is sufficient reason. The

present seems determined to call the lie to
everything in the past" (Henry McBride,
"Demuth," *New York Sun*, April 10, 1926).

Susan Watts Street, who once owned this
work, was a wealthy young New York society
woman whom Demuth first met in Provincetown in 1914. She had frequent contact with
Demuth, visiting him in Paris in 1921, where
she shared an apartment with Beatrice and
Robert Locher; in Morristown, New Jersey,
when he was confined to the sanitorium there;
and in Lancaster. When he died, Demuth left
her a diamond ring. Miss Street eventually
acquired several other works by the artist,
which she bequeathed to Williams College
following her suicide in 1956.

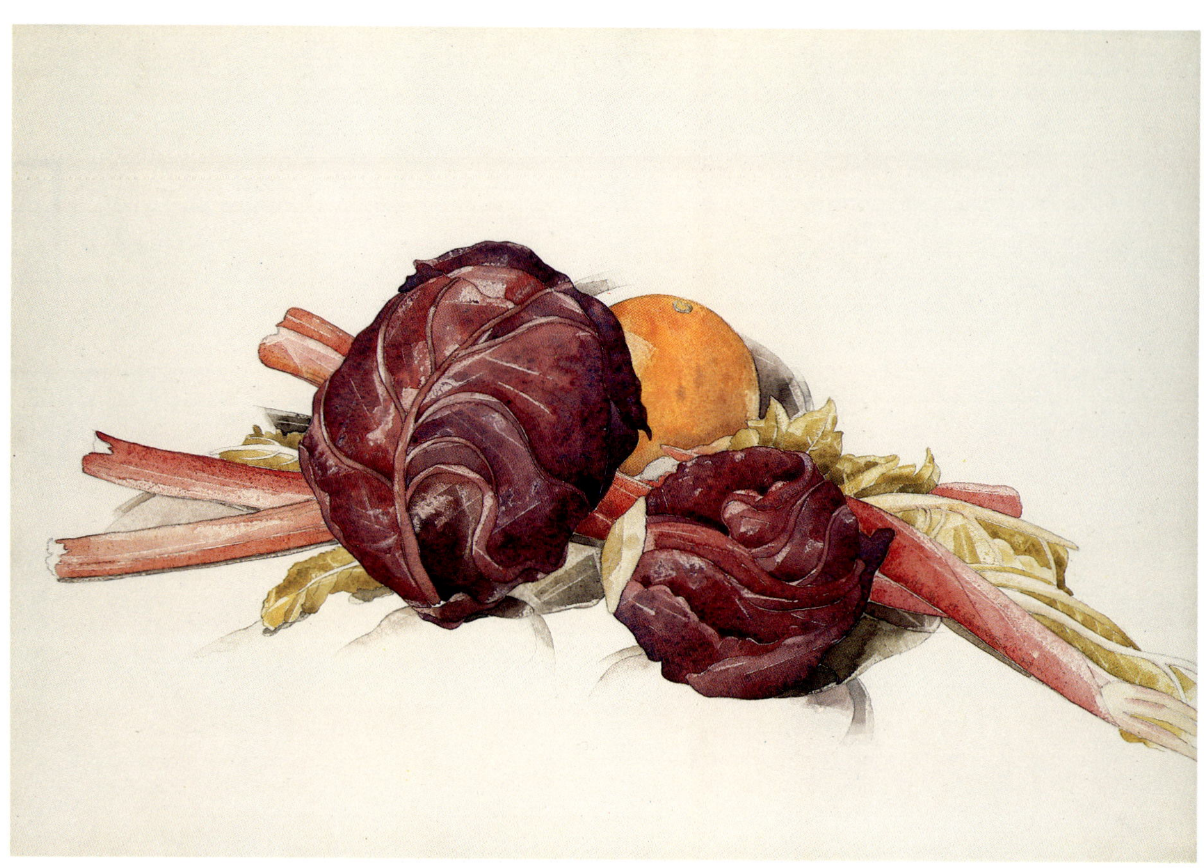

**32. Red Cabbages,
Rhubarb, and Orange,**
1929
Watercolor and pencil on
paper, 14 x 19⅞"
(35.6 x 50.5 cm)

Signed and inscribed,
lower right, in image:
Lancaster, Pa. C. Demuth
'29—

The Metropolitan Museum
of Art, New York. The
Alfred Stieglitz Collection.
49.70.57

Farnham 1959, painting no.
534; Eiseman, no. 9.1929

Provenance: Philip L.
Goodwin, New York;
Alfred Stieglitz, New York,
in exchange for the 1929
watercolor *Green Pears*
(Farnham 1959, painting
no. 527); The Metropolitan
Museum of Art, 1949

Demuth's still lifes were his most popular
works, and their sale accounted for a
substantial portion of the income he received
from galleries. However, his health problems
frequently rendered him unable to paint, as he
complained to Henry McBride: "Have painted
no flowers which means that I'll have less
money next winter" (Demuth to McBride,
August 14, 1927, Henry McBride Papers,
Archives of American Art, Smithsonian
Institution, Washington, D.C.).

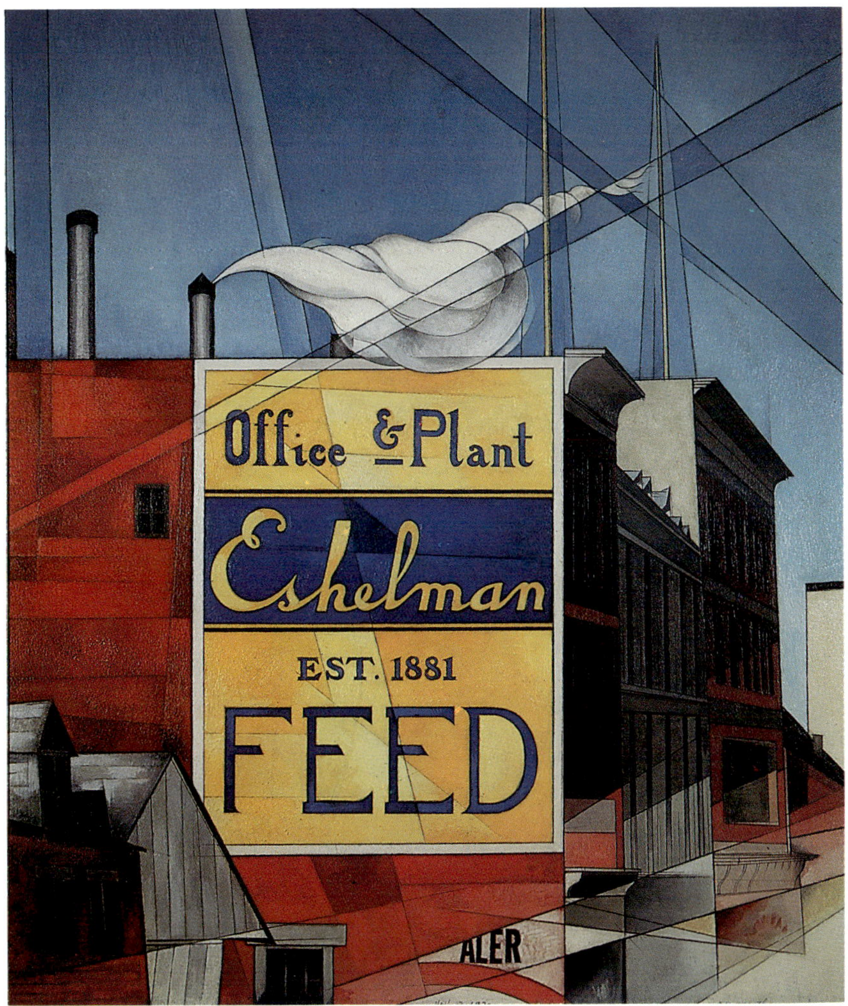

**33. Buildings,
Lancaster,** 1930
Oil on composition board,
24 x 20″ (61 x 50.8 cm)

Signed, lower right:
C. Demuth; inscribed,
lower center: Nov. 13, 1930;
verso: A fragment,
overlooked by Henry
James/who conveniently
named the whole

Whitney Museum of American
Art, New York. Gift of
an Anonymous Donor,
1958. 58.63

Farnham 1959, painting no.
547; Eiseman, no. 1.1930

Provenance: Georgia
O'Keeffe, Abiquiu, New
Mexico, and New York,
1935; Whitney Museum of
American Art, on
permanent loan from
Georgia O'Keeffe, 1953;
Whitney Museum of
American Art, 1958

The buildings that inspired Demuth's painting housed the office and plant of the John W. Eshelman & Sons feed company, established in 1881. They were on North Queen Street in the same block as the grain elevators Demuth depicted in *My Egypt* (no. 29), also owned by the Eshelman company. Although the structures in *Buildings, Lancaster* remain standing today, they have unfortunately been altered beyond recognition by the present owners, Lancaster Association for the Blind.

Typically, Demuth's point of view is elevated from the street level, and he stylizes and flattens the scene, creating a complex pattern of geometric forms. The company's brilliant yellow and blue sign painted on the side of the building provides the dominant visual motif of the scene. As in several other Lancaster scenes, Demuth used strong primary colors, the reds of the brick buildings made even more vibrant by contrast to the sky, where carefully ruled lines function almost like blue search-lights. The yellow poles on the roof and the curling smoke from the chimney further enliven the scene. Although Demuth made illustrations for Henry James's *Turn of the Screw* and "The Beast in the Jungle" in 1918 and 1919, they have no apparent connection to this painting, and the inscription remains unexplained.

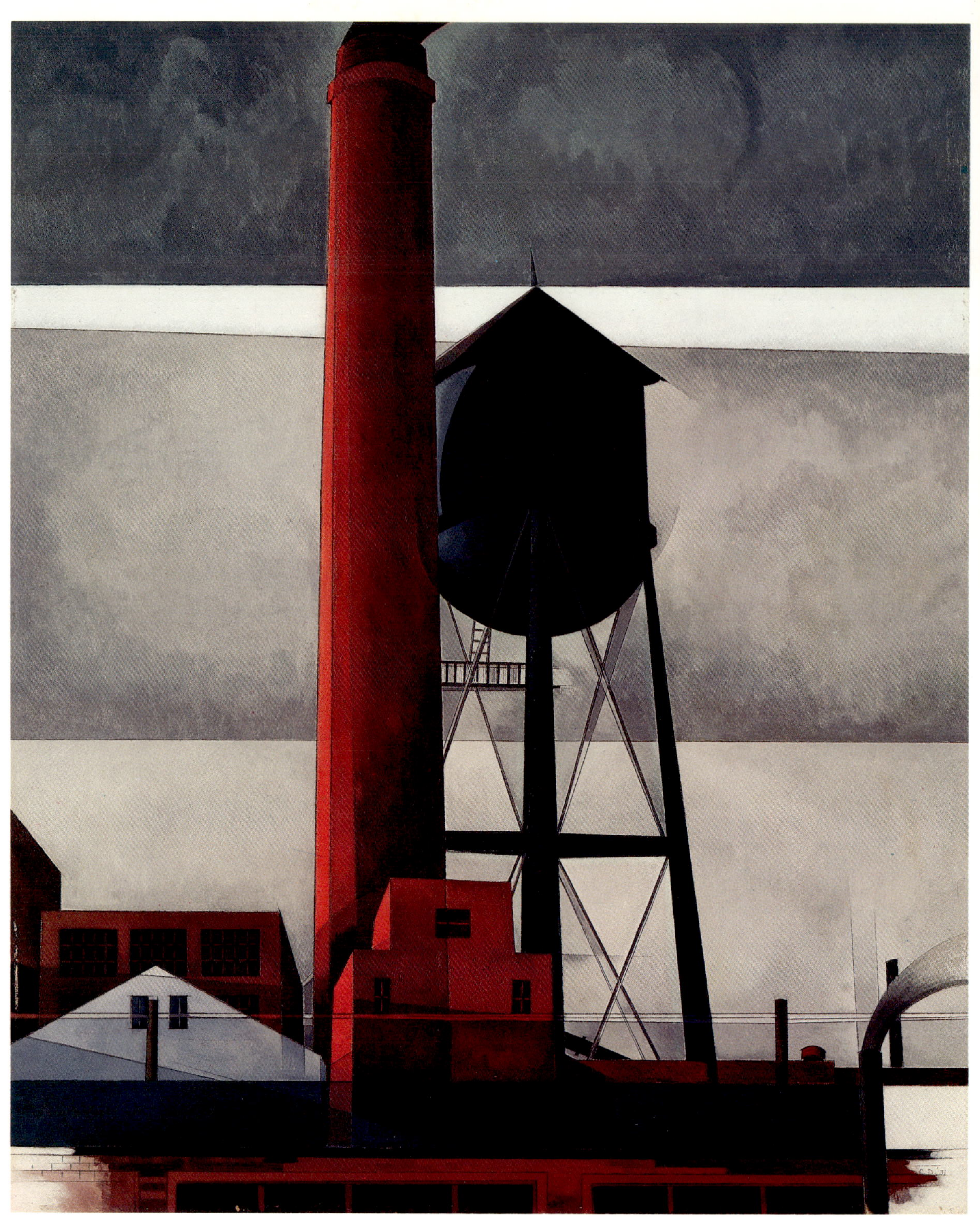

**34. Chimney and
Water Tower,** 1931
Oil on composition
board, 29⅞ x 23⅞"
(75.9 x 60.6 cm)

Signed, lower left: C.D. '31

The Alfred Stieglitz
Collection. Lent to the
National Gallery of Art,
Washington, D.C., by
Georgia O'Keeffe

Farnham 1959, painting no.
553; Eiseman, no. 4.1931

Provenance: Georgia
O'Keeffe, Abiquiu, New
Mexico, and New York,
1935; National Gallery of
Art, Washington, D.C.,
on extended loan, 1949

The architecture of Lancaster provided themes
for Demuth's paintings from 1919 until 1933.
The combination of the sharply vertical forms
of a chimney and the more rounded shape of a
water tower supported on slender legs inspired
several other works, including *Buildings*
(no. 17) and *Aucassin and Nicolette* (no. 19).
As in the case of *Buildings*, the specific
structures that served as the models for this
work have not been identified. The vertical red
of the chimney divides a sky composed of
broad, flat areas of several shades of blue,
dwarfing the architectural forms below. This
was one of several paintings bequeathed at his
death in 1935 to Georgia O'Keeffe, who was a
good friend of Demuth.

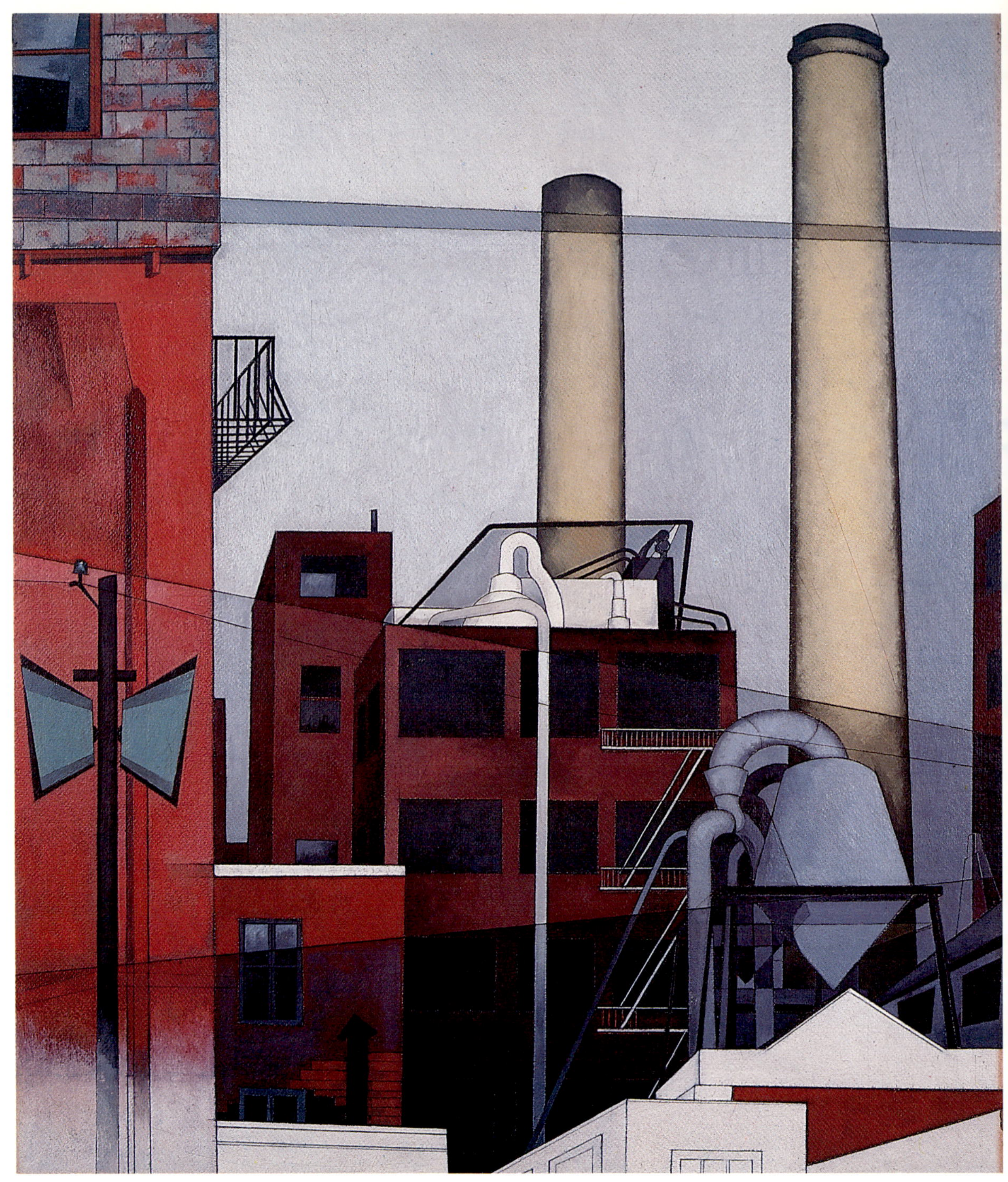

35. "After All," 1933
Oil on composition
board, 36 x 30"
(91.4 x 76.2 cm)

Signed, upper right:
C. Demuth 1933

Norton Gallery and School
of Art, West Palm Beach,
Florida. 53.43

Farnham 1959, painting no.
557; Eiseman, no. 1.1933

Provenance: Georgia
O'Keeffe, Abiquiu, New
Mexico, and New York,
1935; Downtown Gallery,
New York, c. 1950; Ralph
H. Norton, West Palm
Beach, 1952; Norton
Gallery and School of Art,
1953

According to Emily Farnham (Farnham 1959,
p. 635), the source of the title of this work is a
stanza from Walt Whitman's *Leaves of Grass:*
> After all not to create only, or found only,
> But to bring perhaps from afar what is
>   already founded,
> To give it our own identity, average, limitless,
>   free,
> To fill the gross the torpid bulk with vital
>   religious fire,
> Not to repel or destroy so much as accept,
>   fuse, rehabilitate,
> To obey as well as command, to follow more
>   than to lead,
> These also are the lessons of our New
>   World;
> While how little the New after all, how much
>   the Old, Old World!

(Walt Whitman, "Song of the Exposition,"
from *Leaves of Grass*, in *Complete Poetry and
Selected Prose*, edited by James E. Miller, Jr.
[Boston, 1959], p. 142).

The painting was the artist's final work in oil
and his last major architectural piece. While
the buildings upon which Demuth based this
work have not been identified, there are
several factory complexes in Lancaster that
could have served as models.

Henry McBride wrote of just this sort of
view: "His towering smokestacks, relentless
iron girders and violent red bricks are
implacably of this era, and the strange thing
about the manner is that these red bricks and
iron girders, in Mr. Demuth's version of them,
seem beautiful" (Henry McBride, *New York
Herald*, December 17, 1922). This is one of
Demuth's more complex architectural scenes in
its array of buildings, fire escapes, water
towers, and smokestacks. The unusual
structure in the lower right corner of the
painting is a cyclone separator, a kind of
centrifuge widely used in industry. The device
is the dominant visual motif in a 1920 painting
by Demuth, *Machinery (For W. Carlos W.)* (The
Metropolitan Museum of Art; Farnham 1959,
painting no. 385).

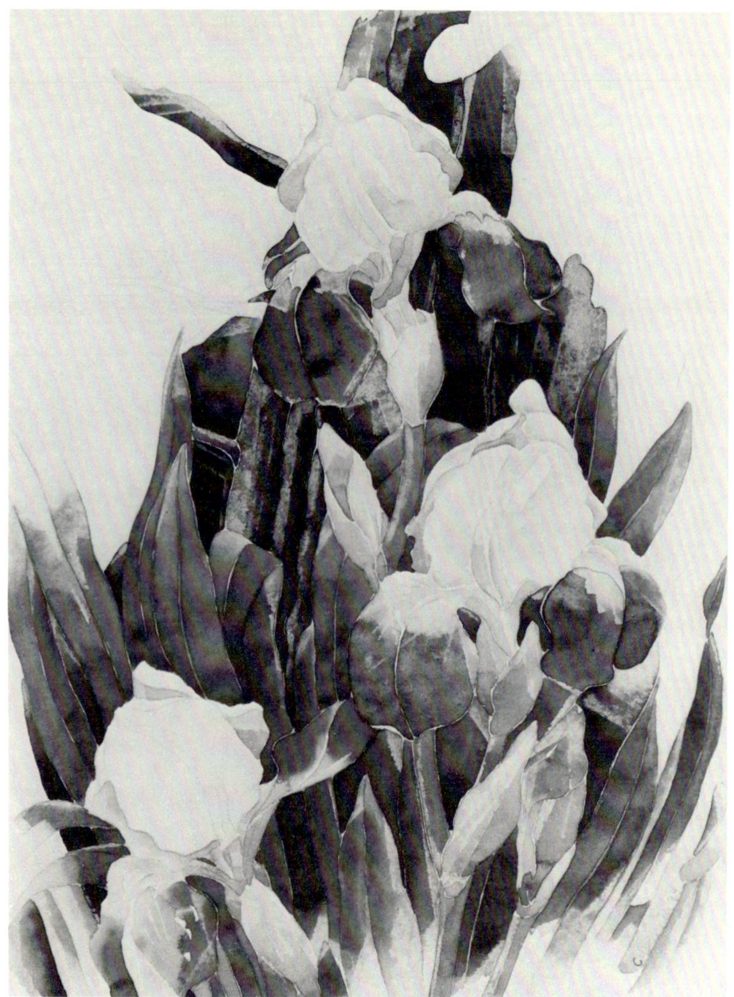

36. Iris, 1933
Watercolor and pencil on
paper, 13¾ x 9½"
(34.9 x 24.1 cm)

Signed, lower right:
C Demuth '33

Erving and Joyce Wolf
Collection

Farnham 1959, painting no.
561; Eiseman, no. 7.1933

Provenance: Augusta B.
Demuth, Lancaster;
Josephine Kieffer (Mrs.
Charles S.) Foltz, Lancaster,
1943; Charles Foltz, Jr.,
Lancaster; Salander-
O'Reilly Galleries, Inc.,
and Davis and Langdale
Co., New York, 1981; Erving
and Joyce Wolf, 1981

Shown only in Philadelphia

The first owner of this work after it left the
Demuth family was Josephine Kieffer Foltz, an
artist and a longtime Lancaster resident. Her
father, Dr. J. B. Kieffer (1838–1910), was
professor of Greek at Franklin and Marshall
College for thirty years and a founding
member of the Cliosophic Society, a Lancaster
organization devoted to intellectual pursuits.

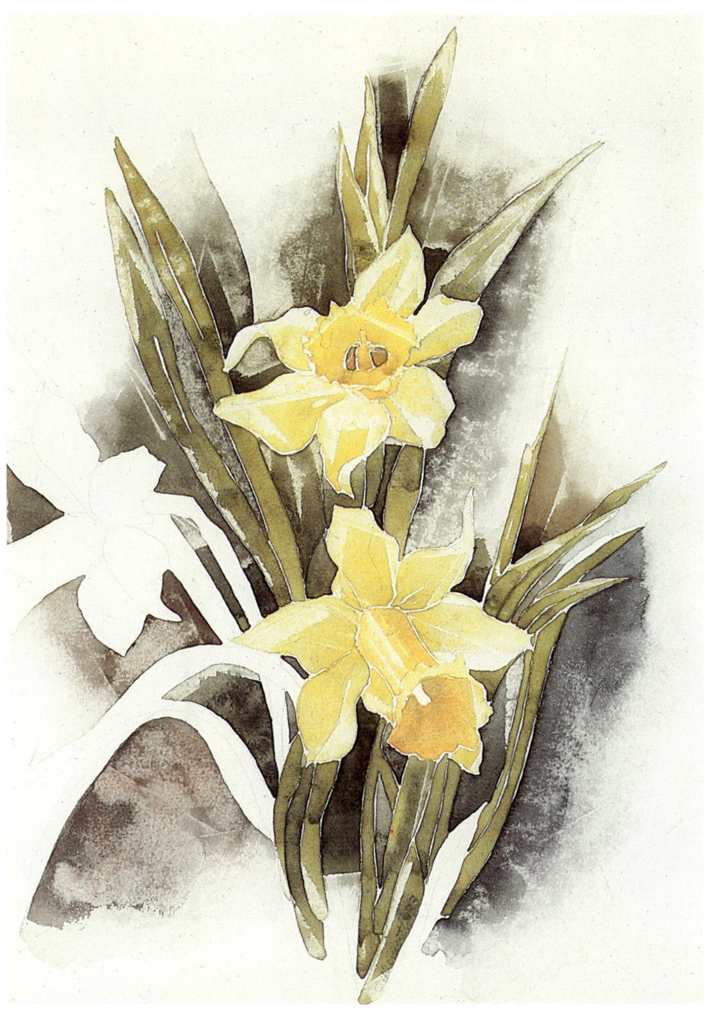

**37. Daffodils
(Jonquils),** 1933
Watercolor and pencil on
paper, 13¹⁵⁄₁₆ x 9¹⁵⁄₁₆"
(35.4 x 25.2 cm)

Signed, lower center, in
image: C. Demuth '33

Private Collection,
Lancaster, Pennsylvania

Farnham 1959, painting no.
562; Eiseman, no. 1.1933

Provenance: Augusta
Demuth, Lancaster;
Lettie Herr (Mrs. John E.)
Malone, Lancaster, 1943;
Mary E. Herr, Lancaster;
private collection, c. 1971

Critics sometimes gave their imaginations free
rein in analyzing Demuth's flower pieces: "In
some mysterious way the whole effect is one of
sinister suggestion—*fleurs du mal,* one feels,
not the innocent blossoms one was led to
expect" (Ritchie 1950, p. 10). An excerpt from a
poem written as a memorial to Demuth by his
friend William Carlos Williams comes closer to
the meaning:

It is miraculous
that flower should rise
by flower
alike in loveliness—
as though mirrors
of some perfection
could never be
too often shown—
silence holds them—
in that space. And
color has been construed
from emptiness
to waken there—

(William Carlos Williams, "The Crimson
Cyclamen [To the Memory of Charles
Demuth]," in *The Collected Earlier Poems of
William Carlos Williams* [Norfolk, Conn.,
1951], p. 397).

Although *Daffodils* at first appears
unfinished, Demuth intended to contrast the
detailed areas of watercolor, the parts that are
merely sketched in with pencil, and the
portions of the page left entirely untouched.

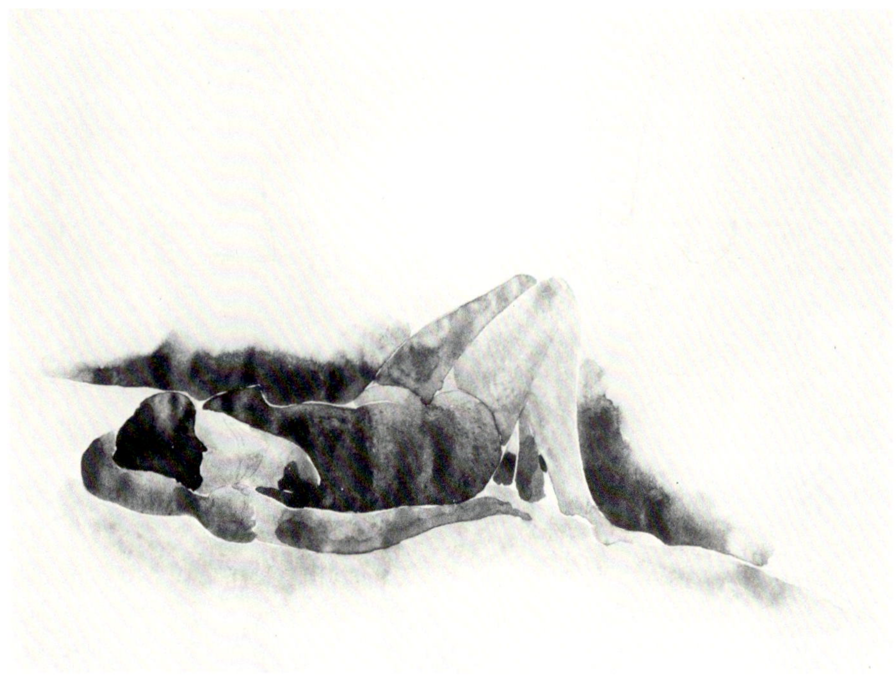

38. Girl Reclining on Beach, Provincetown (Sunburned Figure on Beach), 1934
Watercolor and pencil on paper, 8⅜ x 11"
(21.3 x 27.9 cm)

Private Collection, Lancaster, Pennsylvania

Farnham 1959, painting no. 573; Eiseman, no. 3.1934

Provenance: Robert Locher, Lancaster, 1935; Richard Weyand, Lancaster, 1956; Parke-Bernet Galleries, New York, sale no. 1804, February 5, 1958, lot 77A; private collection, 1958

Demuth's last works were a series of figurative watercolors made on the beach at Province-town, Massachusetts, where he spent the summer of 1934. He was there as the guest of Frank Everts, a Lancaster architect, and his wife Elsie, also an artist, friends he had known in Europe. The Evertses lived at 207 North Lime Street in Lancaster, not far from the house in which Demuth was born, and eventually owned eight works by the artist.

The works that he executed in Provincetown during 1934 reflect a renewed interest in marine themes, which he had not depicted since early in his career. The beach scenes signal a new fluidity in Demuth's work; his sketchbook was ever at hand as he neared the water, and he worked quickly in pencil and colored washes to record the people he saw relaxing on the sand in the shimmering summer light. These little studies represent a final burst of energy for Demuth, a reaffirma-tion of his artistic vision in the face of his rapidly diminishing physical powers.

All photographs were taken or supplied by the owners, except the following: Cover: Salander-O'Reilly Galleries, Inc.; Plates: Will Brown, nos. 1, 2, 6, 10, 11, 30, 37; Geoffrey Clements, no. 29; Michael Cordell, no. 33; Hirschl & Adler Galleries, no. 12; James Maroney, Inc., no. 17; Eric Mitchell, nos. 4, 5, 7, 8, 9, 14, 24; Salander-O'Reilly Galleries, Inc., no. 15; Sotheby Parke Bernet, Inc., no. 3; Figures: Will Brown, fig. 4; John A. Fritz Studio, figs. 8 and 11.

Selected Bibliography and List of Abbreviations for Works Cited

Allara, Pamela. "Charles Demuth: Always a Seeker." *Arts Magazine*, vol. 50, no. 10 (June 1976), pp. 86–89.

Brown 1943–45
Brown, Milton W. "Cubist-Realism: An American Style." *Marsyas*, vol. 3 (1943–45), pp. 138–60.

Brown 1955
Brown, Milton W. *American Painting from the Armory Show to the Depression.* Princeton, 1955.

Celender, Donald Dennis. "Precisionism in Twentieth-Century American Painting." Ph.D. dissertation, University of Pittsburgh, 1963.

Champa, Kermit. "Charlie Was Like That." *Artforum*, vol. 12, no. 7 (March 1974), pp. 54–59.

Cleveland, Ohio. Cleveland Museum of Art. *American Realism and the Industrial Age.* November 12, 1980—January 18, 1981. Also shown at Kenneth C. Beck Center for the Cultural Arts, Lakewood, Ohio, and Columbus Museum of Art.

Davidson, Abraham A. "Cubism and the Early American Modernist." *Art Journal*, vol. 26, no. 2 (winter 1966/67), pp. 122–29, 165.

Davidson, Abraham A. *Early American Modernist Painting, 1910–1935.* New York, 1981.

Demuth 1912
Demuth, Charles. "Aaron Eshelman." *Journal of the Lancaster County Historical Society*, vol. 16, no. 8 (1912), pp. 247–50.

Demuth 1929
Demuth, Charles. "Across a Greco Is Written." *Creative Art*, vol. 5, no. 3 (September 1929), pp. 629–34.

Demuth 1925
Demuth, Henry C. *Demuth's 1770, History of a Lancaster Tradition.* Lancaster, 1925.

Eiseman
Eiseman, Alvord L. *Catalogue Raisonné of the Complete Works of Charles Demuth* (forthcoming).

Eiseman 1976
Eiseman, Alvord L. "A Study of the Development of an Artist: Charles Demuth." Ph.D. dissertation, New York University, 1976.

Eiseman 1982
Eiseman, Alvord L. *Charles Demuth.* New York, 1982.

Faison 1950
Faison, S. Lane, Jr. "Fact and Art in Charles Demuth." *Magazine of Art*, vol. 43, no. 4 (April 1950), pp. 123–28.

Farnham 1959
Farnham, Emily Edna. "Charles Demuth: His Life, Psychology and Works." Ph.D. dissertation, Ohio State University, 1959.

Farnham 1965/66
Farnham, Emily Edna. "Charles Demuth's Bermuda Landscapes." *Art Journal*, vol. 25, no. 2 (winter 1965/66), pp. 130–37.

Farnham 1971
Farnham, Emily Edna. *Charles Demuth: Behind a Laughing Mask.* Norman, Oklahoma, 1971.

Friedman, Martin. "The Precisionist View." *Art in America*, vol. 48, no. 3 (1960), pp. 30–37.

Gallatin 1922
Gallatin, A. E. *American Water-Colorists.* New York, 1922.

Gallatin 1927
Gallatin, A. E. *Charles Demuth.* New York, 1927.

Hartley 1921
Hartley, Marsden. *Adventures in the Arts: Informal Chapters on Painters, Vaudeville, and Poets.* New York, 1921.

Hartley 1936
Hartley, Marsden. "Farewell Charles," in *The New Caravan*, edited by Alfred Kreymborg, Lewis Mumford, Paul Rosenfeld. New York, 1936, pp. 552–62.

Huntington, N.Y. Heckscher Museum. *The Precisionist Painters 1916–1949: Interpretations of a Mechanical Age.* July 7–August 20, 1978.

Lane, James W. "Charles Demuth." *Parnassus*, vol. 8 (March 1936), pp. 8–9.

Lee, Sherman E. "The Illustrative and Landscape Watercolors of Charles Demuth." *Art Quarterly*, vol. 5 (spring 1942), pp. 158–75.

Levy, Herbert S. "Charles Demuth of Lancaster." *Journal of the Lancaster County Historical Society*, vol. 68 (Easter 1964), pp. 41–62.

McBride 1921
McBride, Henry. "Modern Art." *The Dial*, vol. 70, no. 2 (February 1921), pp. 234–36.

McBride 1923
McBride, Henry. "Modern Art." *The Dial*, vol. 74, no. 2 (February 1923), pp. 217–19.

McBride 1929
McBride, Henry. "Water-Colours by Charles Demuth." *Creative Art*, vol. 5, no. 3 (September 1929), pp. 634–35.

McBride 1938
McBride, Henry. "Charles Demuth, Artist." *Magazine of Art*, vol. 31, no. 1 (January 1938), pp. 21–23, 58.

McBride 1975
McBride, Henry. *The Flow of Art: Essays and Criticisms of Henry McBride*. Edited by Daniel Catton Rich. New York, 1975.

Malone, Mrs. John E. "Charles Demuth." *Papers of the Lancaster County Historical Society*, vol. 52, no. 1 (1948), pp. 1–14.

Marling 1980
Marling, Karal Ann. "My Egypt: The Irony of the American Dream." *Winterthur Portfolio*, vol. 15, no. 1 (spring 1980), pp. 25–39.

Minneapolis. Walker Art Center. *The Precisionist View of American Art*. November 13–December 25, 1960. Organized in cooperation with the Whitney Museum of American Art, New York; The Detroit Institute of Arts; Los Angeles County Museum of Art; and San Francisco Museum of Modern Art.

Murrell, William. *Charles Demuth*. New York, 1931.

New York. Whitney Museum of American Art. *Charles Demuth Memorial Exhibition*. December 15, 1937—January 16, 1938.

Norton, Thomas E., ed. *Homage to Charles Demuth, Still Life Painter of Lancaster*. Ephrata, Pa., 1978.

Philadelphia Museum of Art. *Philadelphia: Three Centuries of American Art*. April 11–October 10, 1976. pp. 408–647.

Providence, R. I. Museum of Art, Rhode Island School of Design. *Making Tradition Serve Modernism: The Designs of Robert Locher (1887 [sic]–1956)*. July 28–August 28, 1982.

Ritchie 1950
Ritchie, Andrew Carnduff. *Charles Demuth*. New York, 1950. Catalogue for a retrospective exhibition at the Museum of Modern Art.

Rosenfeld, Paul. "American Painting." *The Dial*, vol. 71, no. 6 (December 1921), pp. 661–70.

Rosenfeld, Paul. "Charles Demuth." *The Nation*, vol. 133 (October 7, 1931), pp. 371–73.

Santa Barbara. The Art Galleries, University of California. *Charles Demuth: The Mechanical Encrusted on the Living*. October 5–November 14, 1971. Also shown at the University Art Museum, University of California, Berkeley; The Phillips Collection, Washington, D.C.; and Munson-Williams-Proctor Institute, Utica, New York.

Smith 1955
Smith, Jacob Getlar. "The Watercolors of Charles Demuth." *American Artist*, vol. 19, no. 5 (May 1955), pp. 26–31, 73.

Soby 1944
Soby, James Thrall. *Contemporary Painters*. New York, 1944.

Stewart 1981
Stewart, Patrick Leonard, Jr. "Charles Sheeler, William Carlos Williams, and the Development of the Precisionist Aesthetic." Ph.D. dissertation, University of Delaware, 1981.

Strand, Paul. "American Water Colors at the Brooklyn Museum." *The Arts*, vol. 2, no. 3 (December 1921), pp. 148–52.

Tashjian 1978
Tashjian, Dickran. *William Carlos Williams and the American Scene, 1920–1940*. New York, 1978.

Tsujimoto, Karen. *Images of America: Precisionist Painting and Modern Photography*. San Francisco, 1982. Catalogue of an exhibition organized by the San Francisco Museum of Modern Art, September 9–November 7, 1982. Also shown at the Saint Louis Art Museum, the Baltimore Museum of Art, Des Moines Art Center, and the Cleveland Museum of Art.

Washington, D.C. National Collection of Fine Arts. *Charles Sheeler*. October 10–November 24, 1968. Also shown at the Philadelphia Museum of Art and the Whitney Museum of American Art, New York.

Watson 1923
Watson, Forbes. "Charles Demuth." *The Arts*, vol. 3, no. 1 (January 1923), pp. 77–78.

Wellman 1931
Wellman, Rita. "Pen Portraits: Charles Demuth, Artist." *Creative Art*, vol. 9, no. 6 (December 1931), pp. 483–84.

Williams 1951
Williams, William Carlos. *The Autobiography of William Carlos Williams*. New York, 1951.

Yale University
New Haven, Conn. Yale University, The Beinecke Rare Book and Manuscript Library. Collection of American Literature.